LONGBOW

Author with his water buffalo on Australia's Melville Island. Taken on the ground at 17 yards with one 1120 grain home-built arrow and a custom-made prototype Black Widow PLX 80# Longbow. Photo by E. Donnall Thomas, Jr.

ADVANCE PRAISE FOR LONGBOW

Campbell ... gives the bows, the animals, and their pursuit the due they deserve, [but] the themes he explores with greatest passion are more complex: divorce, marriage, cancer, family, despair, redemption. [H]e meets these challenges with a sure-footed and thoughtful prose style that would distinguish his work from the field no matter what the topic of the chapter.

E. Donnall Thomas, Jr.
Author, *Have Bow, Will Travel*
Language of Wings

It's rare to find genuine, open-eyed honesty in a "hook and bullet" writer. Even rarer to find a measure of insight into the human condition. But both are here in spades. Longbow is not only the outline of a life well lived, it's also a showcase of damn fine writing. Buy this book. It's a bargain at any price.

Allen Morris Jones
Author, *A Quiet Place of Violence: Hunting and Ethics in the Missouri River Breaks*

I first met Jay Campbell decades ago in a bug infested Florida swamp, longbow in hand. He looks part pirate, part scholar, but he is no closet outdoorsman. He travels the globe as a participant, seeking adventure on less beaten paths, and knows the difference between looking and seeing. To write well is rare, but Campbell writes *vividly* about his outdoor passions, which is rarer still. This book is your ticket to adventure.

Gene Wensel
Award-Winning Author of *Come November* and *Primal Dreams* (DVD).
www.brothersofthebow.com

LONGBOW
A Hunting Life

JAY CAMPBELL

with a foreword by
E. Donnall Thomas, Jr.

Raven's Eye Press
Durango, Colorado

Raven's Eye Press, LLC
Durango, Colorado
www.ravenseyepress.com

Copyright © 2012 Jay Campbell

All rights reserved. This book, or parts thereof, may not be reproduced in any form without permission from the author.

Campbell, Jay.
 Longbow: A Hunting Life/Jay Campbell
 p. cm.

1. Hunting
2. Travel
3. Adventure
4. Wildlife
I. Title

ISBN: 978-0-9840056-0-4
LCCN: 2011938787

Cover design by John Reid Campbell
Cover photo by E. Donnall Thomas, Jr.
Interior design by Lindsay J. Nyquist, *elle jay design*
Photography by Jay Campbell unless otherwise indicated

Printed in the United States of America
1 3 5 7 9 10 8 6 4 2

Find out more about Jay Campbell at jaycampbellphotography.com

TABLE OF CONTENTS

Foreword, *by E. Donnall Thomas Jr.* xiii
Introduction xv
They Shoot Pigs, Don't They?. 1
Isla Mona 9
Last Run Down the Moose John 19
Molokai Madness. 27
Last Trip with the Old Man 33
The Closet 39
Back in the Black Water 43
The End of the Northern Road 47
Finding Will. 53
Drowning in the Sag 63
A Goat Too Far 73
Easy Does It. 79
Karen's Heart. 85
When Fish Fly. 91
Virgil's Lion 99
Prodigal Nimrod 107
Prescription: Buffalo 115
Looking for Mister Goodbear 127
Lady Gator. 135
Jukebox. 145
Got Gator?. 153
Red Sky at Night. 161
Coons, Cuisine, and Counterinsurgency. 165
Hopelessly Helping. 173

Bonus: Chapter One
Archer's Paradox, a novel
(expected Fall 2013)

Archer's Paradox. 183

LONGBOW

DEDICATION

To **KAREN**,
who made my life worth living, and then saved it.

Longbow

Acknowledgments

To my friends and gifted writers Don Thomas, Gene Wensel, Allen Jones, and Jay Massey (Jay passed on soon after our time together), thank you. You were always ahead of me, but took the time to slow down, reach out a hand, and pull me along. I appreciate the friendship and effort more than I can express.

From Karen and me to our seven sons and daughters, some of whom tolerate us, and to our grandchildren and grandchildren-to-be: we love you and our doors are always open.

To our constant companions - Mountain Man Butch Wilks, the Reverend Scotty Bennett, Sensei "Alligator Don" Davis, Surfing Chef Chip Turknett, Camp Cook Craig Courty and our South African Redneck Gator Guide Chris Horsman: Thank you for your guidance, food, friendship, and for sharing our adventures.

To O.L. Adcock, who custom crafted two 70-pound longbows for Karen's buffalo hunt, and to Ken Beck at Black Widow Bows, who custom crafted two 80-pound longbows for me.

And to Lois and Reid, my mom and dad, who showed me by example how, and more importantly how not, to live.

Some of the stories within were published in earlier forms, as noted below:

> Jukebox, *Gray's Sporting Journal*
> Lady Gator, *Sports Afield*
> The Closet, *The Chattahoochee Review*
> Karen's Heart and Isla Mona, *Bowhunter Magazine*
> Molokai Madness, *Canadian Bowhunter Magazine*
> Archer's Paradox, *The Professional Bowhunter Magazine*

Many of the remaining stories were first published in *Traditional Bowhunter Magazine* by my long time editor, Don Thomas.

Foreword

by E. Donnall Thomas, Jr.

Most books about bowhunting fall predictably into one of two categories: instruction (often to remarkably little benefit) and thinly disguised attempts to glorify the writer's accomplishments in the field. Readers should expect very little of either in this volume from Jay Campbell, and be glad of it.

Plenty of bowhunting lies between these covers to be sure, from venues as diverse as Alaska and Australia to the Caribbean and, above all, the Florida swamps Jay and his wife Karen have grown to love. The whitetail deer that form a staple of the genre are notable by their scarcity, replaced by the likes of water buffalo, alligators, and feral hogs. This disregard for convention and enthusiasm for diversity no doubt reflects the author's own eclectic background, for at various times he has been a medic, fireman, police officer, surgical PA, rock drummer, attorney, and head of a business specializing in procurement of organs for transplantation. Even if the specifics of bowhunting subject matter were the only consideration, the reader would be unlikely to encounter a "bowhunting" book like this one for some time to come.

But Jay Campbell's departure from cliché in this book runs even deeper. While he gives the bows, the animals, and their pursuit the due they deserve, the themes he explores with greatest passion are more complex: divorce, marriage, cancer, family, despair, redemption. Throughout all, archery and the outdoors emerge as the pole toward which his internal compass swings, a beacon of reliability in a life that sometimes needs it badly indeed, as all worthwhile lives sometimes do.

As a writer, he meets these challenges with a sure-footed and thoughtful prose style that would distinguish his work from the field no matter what the topic of the chapter. This is his first book on any subject. The reader can only hope there will be more.

E. Donnall Thomas, Jr.
Lewistown, MT
June 2011

Introduction

I'm in my middle years as this book is released. It's a hard time for men, our middle years. We face the cold truth of our lives. We measure what we've done against what is left to do, with one eye on the clock. Some are happy and stay the course. Some cheapen their time chasing trophies. But some, like me, are chastened and change direction.

At fifty I quit my job and left my home. I took my longbow and my books and not much more. Friends said I had lost my senses. I might have. But the home fires had died and my life had to change. I moved to the mountains. I took back my senses. I started over.

This book grew from the ashes of that prescribed burn. I began to hunt and write from a new perspective. I found my wife Karen. And I chased adventure with the longbow as if it was my salvation. It may have been.

I had surgery for cancer just after Karen and I married. We decided to bet on adventure as the cure for what ailed me. We doubled down on my earlier expeditions to Isla Mona, the Arctic Ocean, Molokai and the Moose John River (all of which are here, in the book's first chapters). With one eye on the clock and the other on my cancer, we carried our longbows to Australia's Tiwi Islands, the Yukon, New Mexico's mountains, and our beloved Florida swamps. We've had a good start.

Five years from surgery I'm cancer-free. Karen, who started from scratch as a hunter and archer, has hunted bear, elk, alligator, and Barbary sheep. She is the first woman to take a water buffalo with a longbow, as far as we know. Those stories are also here, in the book's later chapters.

Adventure and excitement have their place, to be sure. I can't chase anything with a longbow and not feel a thrill. But thrills need perspective. The how and why of hunting is more important than the what, or the where, or with whom. I have tried to bring that perspective to these pages along with excitement. The perspective that in hunting - as in life - the joy is in the journey. The outcome is an afterthought.

This book is for Karen, who saved my life.

Jay Campbell
Tampa, Florida
July 2011

They Shoot Pigs, Don't They?

Just north of the Florida Everglades, the town of Palmdale lies beside State Road 27 like a dog with a broken back. People drive by and shake their heads, but they don't stop. If the town ever had a prime, it's past it. On the map Palmdale marks a spot between Winterhaven and Belle Glade, but on the road it's hard to tell where it starts and stops. It's a bad place to come for fuel or food, a poor place to hunt, and a good place to leave behind. But our time and wallets were tight, we wanted to hunt Florida pigs, and it was the best we could afford.

The only store in town is the Ice Cream Shoppe, which sold gas until a Kenworth bound for Tampa crushed the pumps under a load of oranges. There was no fire, which really is a shame. The ice cream smelled like diesel until the new flavors came in, but most of the business there is in video games, deep-fried spuds, and chicken. It's a quick stop for quick food for anyone unlucky enough to be hungry forty-eight miles from the nearest McDonalds. Which was me and Danny Hawke.

This hunt was a bottom-of-the-barrel, low-budget deal, a do-it-yourself chance to find game on a tract of private pasture and swampland, no guarantees. Our directions had the Ice Cream Shoppe down as the last landmark in civilization. We stopped, held our breath in the outdoor Port-O-Let, bought some fried chicken and ice, and followed our map to a cow pasture gate. There we waited for our cowman contact to bring the keys to the swamp and lead us in. We paid a small cash fee, followed his truck a few miles through cow pastures, piney woods, and oak bottoms, and stopped in a stand of oaks surrounding a hand pump for water.

"Set them tents up here," our host said, "and I'll come fetch you in two days. You can't get in or out until then, so try not to get hurt. It's hot, boys. You find water, you'll find hogs. Try walking north a ways."

And that was that. It was hot, too. In an hour or so we had tents set up and were sweating through our camo jeans and T shirts. A map nailed to a tree, covered in plastic, gave a good idea of where the water was, so we split up and agreed to meet back at camp after dark. Not that we really knew all that much about the Florida swamps or hog hunting. In fact, we were just a couple of city boys who got excited about hunting with longbows and figured we'd give it a try. Overall, it was probably better that we didn't know what we were doing, or we might not have tried to do it.

Danny Hawke and I were two middle-aged men in middle-management, looking for something interesting to do. Danny has a lot of American Indian blood, and did a tour in the army rangers. I have a little American Indian blood, and did a tour through the sixties. We'd both had interesting times years ago until life began to grind us down. Chasing wild pigs through the Everglades with wooden bows and arrows seemed a sure cure for what ailed us.

A chance encounter with legendary longbow man Dan Quillian had set us on the traditional track. On a business trip to Georgia we saw Dan's Archery Traditions sign near a shopping mall in Athens. We pulled in because of my lifelong interest in archery, and soon Dan was telling us about the homemade electroshock treatments that were healing his diabetic leg. Hearing about a fellow plugging himself into a 110 volt outlet every night made chasing pigs seem tame, so we bought a couple of Longhunter bows and all the accessories. We were off.

After a few months of practice and telephone conversations with Dan about shooting and hunting we decided we could shoot well enough to hunt. Whether we could hunt well enough to shoot remained to be seen. But after a trip to the Wal-Mart for hunting clothes, we booked the low budget adventure, and that brings us back to Palmdale and the swamp.

The Florida swamp spills out from black water streams in the wet season, covering cypress trunks to the level of a man's head. High water marks tell the stories of wet years and dry years like the pencil

Author with a pitch black Florida swamp boar.
Photo by Karen Campbell.

marks on door frames that measure children. As I eased into the lowlands, it was dry season, winter, and much more land was available to walk than usual. I looked up at the high water marks from years past then down at gouged-out gator holes that were normally sunken under deep water. The bottom muck was firm enough, but oozed a musty smell. My boots sank in and sucked free with a slorping sound. Spanish moss is a soft gentle plant that gives the darkening swamp a mysterious look. It billowed from branches like grey lace curtains. It was a spooky place, made more so by the swoop and whoosh of owls setting off to hunt, rousted from their beds by my evening walk.

The night's stroll showed rooting ruts and tracks of hogs, and sign of gators, deer, turkey, and even big snakes on the sandy roadbeds. I walked from camp toward a black rivulet cutting into a cypress grove. It still held running water. I turned along the stream bed, walking gently and slowly, following cues from hunting magazines and videos. I hadn't done anything like this since I was twelve, and then I was chasing rabbits in the snow, which really didn't qualify. Heeding video advice to "walk as slow as you can, then cut your speed in half," I soon heard a noise. It barely broke the swamp silence. A grinding noise, like you feel in your head when chewing an ice cube. This wasn't an animal sign I had read about anywhere. I followed the noise slowly to its source, a clump of reeds in the middle of a slough. A Florida slough is a cross between a pond, a ditch, and a bog, and might better be described as a wet, mucky clearing. This one held water, and something in its reedy center was breaking bones or chewing carrots. I had no idea what it was or which of those things it was doing, but I plunged in.

As it turned out, this particular slough held plenty of water, so I could wade toward the reeds without making noise. On the other hand, the closer I got to the noise, the deeper the water became. When I was up to my waist I started thinking much more about alligators than pigs. I saw the pig then, a wild Florida boar, standing up to its neck in the dark water, eyes happily closed, grinding its teeth and tusks together while munching on reeds and roots it was pulling up from the bottom. I was stunned, to be so wet and so close to such a big mammal. I squatted down until we both seemed to be swimming in the reeds, not ten yards apart. Everything I was carrying was underwater except the bow and the arrows on my bow quiver.

I did not seem in danger of being found out. It was nearly dark and I was hidden from the bristly submariner by river cane and the noise of his grinding tusks. Even so, under the circumstances, I wished for a harpoon or torpedo more than a bow. *Call me Ishmael*, I thought, as I debated whether I should smite the beast above or below the waterline. As they often do (I have since learned), the pig made up my mind for me, and waded a few steps to higher ground. When his chest was cut neatly in half by the black water I had a target. From two fathoms away I rose out of the muck and shot with the bow heeled over hard, keeping the lower limb out of the water. The arrow struck the pig amidships, and he breached the calm water's surface like a marlin. If I had hooked him to a two-hundred-pound line I might have played him in. But he tacked to shallow water and left the dark pool for the palmetto jungle. It was a neat amphibious trick, one that any marlin would envy. I was left alone waist deep in the cool water, watching a moonlit trail of bubbles and broken cane leading to my Moby Dick. It was suddenly very, very, quiet.

My arrow was floating on the surface, and had obviously passed through the pig. This I took for a good sign. A slick of blood was on the water. It wasn't hard to wade to dry land following the trail. Then things changed. I found a few drops of blood heading toward the jungle's edge, but no more. And I really wasn't sure exactly where the pig had entered the heavy growth. I'd been just a little excited after the shot, and hadn't marked the spot. I used up the limited life in my flashlight trying to find drops of blood, then figured I needed help. I marked the last drop, then went for lanterns and Danny Hawke, my Indian tracker.

In *Northwest Passage* Spencer Tracy plays Major Robert Rogers, the man who created the first band of army rangers as well as "Rogers's Rules" of irregular warfare. These are still used by the Rangers today. Tracy warns his rangers about the bloodthirsty Abenaki Indians, which always gives me a swell of pride. My French Trader great-great-Grandfather named Brown married an Abenaki woman named Kerranapuk, on my mother's side. This might account for the occasional burst of hatefulness on my part (if Rogers is to be believed) but it hasn't proved to be worth spit when it comes to tracking and other hunting skills. Danny Hawke has much more Native American blood than I do and so, by genetic rights, ought to be dandy at tracking and hunting. But he isn't worth much either. Hunting skills, it seems, are not a dominant trait in the gene pool. Or there's a lot more nurture than nature involved in the process. Either way, we had a couple of folks heading out after dark in the Florida Swamp, holding big lanterns in shaky hands, trying to track a wounded pig without a smidgen of acquired or inbred talent.

"What'll we do?" Danny asked, when I told him my story.

"Track him down," I said lightly. I acted confident while I helped fill the lanterns and check the mantles.

"What about snakes?" He had a good point.

"They're asleep," I countered, trying to remember my Discovery Channel education about cottonmouths and rattlesnakes. Unfortunately, I began to remember that snakes generally feed at night in the swamps. I thought that was information I should best keep to myself, at least if I wanted to count on any Indian tracker services before morning.

Like a prisoner-chase scene from *Cool Hand Luke*, we rustled and banged gear together in the truck, driving rope, lanterns, come-alongs, knives, bone saws, hoists, snake-bite kits and extra gas as close as we could to the spot where I had seen the last blood. Then we lurched out along the trail in the dark, lanterns swaying, the two of us alternately whispering and shouting. I couldn't recall whether being quiet was supposed to be as important when tracking as when hunting, and the whispering made things kind of spooky. Soon we were lying on the ground, singeing our face-hairs on the lanterns, staring at grains of sand and shoots of grass from inches away, trying to find drops of blood. In an hour or so we had belly-crawled forty yards into the palmetto jungle, pushing the lanterns ahead of us. In two hours we had covered nearly one hundred yards, microdrop by microdrop. Then the trail just stopped. Dead.

In later years, I would learn that this can happen when an animal's heart shuts down, even though beasts can still make a few more yards on attitude and momentum. But we were stumped. And we were spooked, a lot spooked, lying there under the lowest palmetto cover with the lanterns projecting up into our faces as if we were gravediggers in a horror movie. So it was natural to react the way we did when Danny yanked a palmetto frond loose and a bloody, bristly, boogered-up boar's head flopped down between our faces.

Middle-aged middle managers should not be exposed to such messy things in the middle of the night. The risk of sudden death is significant. The commotion upsets the ecosystem. Al Gore would not approve. Needless to say, we separated ourselves from the boar's head at a high rate of speed bulldozing a two-lane track out of the palmettos. It was easy to follow that track later, much later, when we returned. After a jumpy time spent poking the pig with sticks, we dragged it back to camp and a waiting winch and gambrel. With coolers full of good meat, the next day we followed our host back to Route 27, leaving him behind as we turned north to Tampa. We passed through Palmdale again, but this time we didn't stop.

Today Palmdale is still little more than an accumulation of oil on the highway where cars and trucks slow down before thinking better of it. The hunting there has been converted to caged boar hunts. This first hunt happened many years ago, and began my love of hunting wild places with primitive bows. In truth, I am no more comfortable in the woods today than I was then. Although I have trucked longbows and selfbows to a score of states to hunt a bundle of animal species, I have had limited success if a game pole is the measuring stick. But I do not propose another measure. I don't think of myself as an accomplished hunter or woodsman. I am neither. I struggle to find time to escape the obligations of city life and the office, and count myself lucky when I do. Each time I enter the wilds, whether mountains, tundra, or swamps, I know I am outmatched, unprepared, and at risk. But that is what attracts me to the hunt and the wild places from my comfortable home in the city—the chance to learn again that only I am responsible for my actions and their consequences, and that sometimes nothing I do can prepare me for nature's quirks.

For me, hunting in primitive places with the most primitive of weapons brings me closest to this truth. And for that I am grateful to Palmdale, which otherwise has nothing on this earth to recommend it. It was the place my journey began.

Isla Mona

The stewardess smelled like sweet smoke and her eyes were the color of island coffee. When she leaned in her blouse strained against its buttons, and if I wasn't already going to Puerto Rico I would have changed my flight just to follow her home. She asked where I was going, but pushed me away when I told her: *Isla Mona*. "Vampires on that island," she snapped, and turned her considerable Latin heat toward the next man in line.

I couldn't blame her. The Miami headlines had shouted it all morning: "*Chupacabra* kills sixteen more on Isla Mona." The legendary vampire goatsucker was making my life difficult before I even left the ground. But there were lots more goats on Mona Island for the Chupacabra to eat or drain of blood or whatever it did, so eight Angelo boys from the mainland were safe, the way I saw it. Still, I kept the news to myself. It wouldn't do for someone to quit this Carribean goat hunting expedition until their share of the boat and hotel bills had been paid. I settled back in my seat for the long flight to Puerto Rico, the most unlikely of hunting destinations.

The next morning my friends and I left the fishing village of

Boqueron, Puerto Rico for Mona Island. It was fifty miles across the restless Mona Passage, over some of the deepest water in the world. The *Orca Too* was our ship, stocked with hundreds of gallons of water and ice to unload on the beach. Mona allows nothing to outsiders, not even a drink. You pack your own gear and water or you don't get off the boat.

The crossing was rough. The captain asked that we get sick over the railing to keep his deck clean. I was unprepared for seasickness, but it had been hard to prepare for much about Mona, as so few people had ever been there. The Fodor's travel guide hinted why, describing our trip across the "shark-infested Mona passage." I moved sharks ahead of vampires on my worry list.

It had taken me five years to talk seven adventurous archers into this trip, but I was beginning to rethink the idea. Heaving on the Orca's deck in the dark, and rethinking the trip as well, were Doctor Jose DeMoya, bowyer Steve Hohensee, young Ben Pinney, buffalo hunter Rick McGowan, Missourians Dennis and Crystal Harper, and diver Clayton Smith. I finally slept, leaving my fate to the captain and his compass. But when the sun burst full in the sky I was jolted awake by cheers. Isla Mona was illuminated.

She looked worth the celebration. Mona is a sheer column of cave-pocked rock shooting two hundred feet straight from the sea, screaming of adventure. Jungle greens hang from her high ledges. Crystal beaches wrap the blue pools at her bottom. *Pirates and plunder*, I thought to myself, as salt spray bit my face. The weight of a cutlass was nearly real on my belt. I warmed to the role, but the shouting on deck snapped me back to the moment. Voices debated Mona's past, what little was known of it, and how the goats and pigs we came to chase got there. I dropped the dream of a cutlass and joined in.

Mona is deserted now but for a squad of rangers, though in the past she was explored and exploited until one couldn't be told from the other. Taino natives gave way to Columbus, and Columbus to Spanish sailors. The sailors gave way to pirates, and pirates to business, but nothing succeeded on Mona. Captain Kidd hid in the island's honeycombed caves, but was hanged before he could return for his treasure. Guano mining, tree farming, and cattle ranching all failed. Only one enterprise has ever thrived on Mona: the foreign herds of goats and pigs we had come to hunt. Hundreds of years ago sailors loosed mating pairs for a renewable food source on the island. These became feral herds that can't be exterminated, so have to be culled. A hunting season was the government's solution, but more than that we did not know. We would have to learn about Isla Mona for ourselves once we left the Orca's shifting deck for the steady feel of sand.

The Orca moored in a blue lagoon off a white sand beach under coconut palms. Fish schooled in the cove. The sun burned, but breezy nights were forecast. We had two days to play on the beach before hunting season began, but Jose and I set our tents, stored our gear, and climbed to the highlands to scout for goats. We had come to hunt.

What we found up there was another planet: acrid, hostile, and impossibly overgrown. A storm had blown most of the palms into miles of logjam. We searched for game and water and found neither. There was no sign of goats. Cactus pads hitched themselves to our clothes and lanced our skin. Every step brought a new kind of pain. We retreated to nurse our blisters and salve our wounds.

In the morning, the lowlands were more inviting. The sand flats were laced with open trails. There was no goat sign, but pig rooting was evident. Still, there were no animals seen. Eight experienced hunters were frustrated and confused. But if the hunting was poor, the fishing and gathering were outstanding. Clayton struck schools of blue runners for dinner, and waded for octopus. Coconuts were easy to knock down, with the meat of the nut still sweet and pudding-soft like a

Dr. Jose De Moya glassing on Puerto Rico's Isla Mona island (Eiffel's lighthouse in the background).

custard. Conch and cactus fruit were everywhere. But eating - any kind of eating - attracted Mona's giant iguanas.

The five foot lizards are protected, which is the only thing that kept us from killing them all. The rustle of food wrappers brought them like coyotes to road kill, and they bit our toes as often as scraps. We pelted them with coconuts and hermit crabs to keep them at a distance, and in part, to keep ourselves from being bored. Until day three.

"Things change so fast," young Ben said. He was spinning stories about the Spanish goats he and Steve had ambushed on the beachside cliffs. We crowded in to listen.

"We were done hunting, napping on the beach, when a string of goats was skylined on the cliffs."

I interrupted. "Damn, Ben. Those cliffs are fifty yards up, and a quarter-mile from the beach." I ran my hands over the caped-out horns and rich dark meat spread out on a tarp.

"Yeah, but Steve and I just hacked through that thick bush and climbed up."

Steve was sweating hard and pretending to be asleep, but he spoke up with his eyes still closed. "We went hand over hand up the wall until we reached the top ledge. Dennis waved us toward the goats from the beach."

"Did they all have horns?" Jose asked. He liked this cliff-climbing idea for goats. It was a nice set of horns they packed back, the curved brown crown of a mature feral goat. I wanted to taste the burgundy meat and hear the whole story. Once Steve and Ben had clawed their way up the cliff, they found a band of wild goats about eighty pounds each. Working as a team they put fatal arrows through the same big billy, although the retrieve took them on hands and knees deep into a cliff-side cave. They made the two hour hike back to camp by late afternoon, and they weren't the only hunters with good news.

Clayton and Rick stumbled back from the highlands with a story. "I missed," Rick said, "a big, black pig at twenty yards." The miss, he explained, was a result of lightheadedness from a head injury. "But you won't believe what we found," he went on. "A mile farther than any of us have been, everything changes! There's more animal sign than I've ever seen anywhere, everywhere! You can't walk without stepping in it, and the bush opens up to beautiful country for stalking."

Clayton nodded his head. "Dude, that's not all! There are caves up there. Caves like I've never seen. One's a hundred yards wide and you can walk underground until the cave opens out to the ocean. There's stalagmites, stalactites and animal bones scattered in the dust. It's kind of spooky!"

The game was afoot. Goats, pigs, caves—all the exotic promises of Isla Mona were coming together with two days left to hunt. Neither Rick nor Clayton wanted to go back on top. They were exhausted. But I was rested and Steve had an idea.

"That cave," he said. "Go up and camp in that cave tonight and hunt first thing. Save yourself a three hour hike in the dark."
Dennis and I put kits together for a night out—sleeping pads, three gallons of water each, cold dinners. Crystal made me promise to bring the big man back and I solemnly swore it. Three hours later we broke out of thick bush into a long scrub plain on the edge of the sea cliffs. Rick was right—fresh sign was everywhere. But we couldn't find the cave and it was almost dark. How could we miss a hole in the ground one hundred yards wide?

It is the nature of mysterious places to remain mysterious. No self-respecting pirate cave should give up its secrets without a struggle. Some use hidden chambers, snake-filled pits, or swarms of bats to protect their mysteries. Others, like this one, employ only camouflage. Clayton had fallen into this cave while looking for a little bathroom privacy. The ground suddenly slipped away and slid him into a hole two stories high, completely hidden from the surface. Even with instructions we found it accidentally, casting about until the ground fell away from us in the jungle growth.

Every step beneath the surface peeled away our years. We became raw, scared boys like Huck and Tom watching out for Pap and Injun Joe. We stumbled through chambers of every size, some inspiring, others suffocating. Stalactites and limestone columns led to open windows on the ocean. We stood looking down with our mouths open, smiling, speechless, dizzy. Then we stoked a bonfire and tended it well, talking through the night. We were too excited, and maybe too scared, to close our eyes in that spooky pit. Come morning, we left the cave as we found it: clean, hidden, looming, awesome.

At dawn we climbed from the cave hand over hand, and picked our way through rock fields toward the ocean cliffs. A brightening sky revealed more animal sign than I had ever seen. Scat and tracks were layered in all directions, and grunts and clacking hooves sounded close by. Dennis and I separated, each trailing our own herd of hogs.

Pigs' hooves rang on hollow stones, and led me to the cliff's edge. Far below me the sun warmed Isla Monita, Mona's misty little sister. Then the ground beneath my feet began to vibrate. Lights flashed from below. The vibration became a noise, then a rush of air as an intruder thumped into view from below the cliff. A helicopter rose to eye level, the military pilot hanging in the dawn as he assessed my camouflage clothes and weapon. Apparently satisfied I was not a terrorist, he gave me a crisp salute and banked away. *Of all the times and places,* I thought.

The pounding blades had scattered my pigs. I sat on the ledge and looked down on the blue passage. Sea birds looped in and out of the caves underneath. Up here were Taino pictographs, all that's left of the natives who looked down from these same cliffs when Columbus came. I was lost in Mona's blue haze, Taino natives painting my thoughts, when a persistent sound worked its way into my head. it was a munching sound with the regular clack of tusks. A feeding boar hog. I chased the noise until thick brush gave way to low grass. A dark shape tore at the scrub, a Spanish pig with flopping black ears and a shaggy black coat. He was feeding inland, the ocean protecting his back. I crawled within eight yards, hands and knees on the flat volcanic rock. He never saw me. I took a breath, found the hair I would focus on, and drew back my Osage bow. I remember thinking, "he's so close—I should hold low," just before I sent a river cane arrow under his chest where it burst apart on the rocks. Eight yards.

For the second time in a day I stood with my mouth open, disbelieving. The pig woofed and cantered off, his head craned back toward the ocean that had betrayed him. I watched him go and thought of five years of planning and three days of highland torture spent for one perfect opportunity. Five years.

The heat of the day was building. I gathered my shattered arrow and set out to find Dennis and head to camp. It was a long, hot hike back and I pushed the pace beyond my reserves and his, angry at myself, tired to my bones. It wasn't fair to Dennis, but I hoped he understood.

On the last day I was all played out, ready for a mainland bath and a meal. My companions were beat down and ready to call it a trip. But Mona doesn't let go so easily. After dinner Steve and Ben took snorkels and spears to the lagoon while the rest of us shooed iguanas and cleaned dishes. Crystal half-joked, "Of course Steve's gone with dishes to do." Which got us thinking—where was Steve? And more importantly, where was Ben?

We ran to the dock, then to the beach. One figure crawled from the water. It was Ben, and he was upset. "I can't find Steve," he gasped. "We got separated and I've been looking out there for half an hour." Jeez. "Out there" was past the reef, in the Mona Passage, after dark. Sharks. And if the current caught him, he'd be on his way to Santo Domingo. All hell broke loose. We went for lights, boats, and Rangers.

"You know, *compadre*," the Ranger Captain said as his searchlight flashed the water, "a yellowtail stingray might have got your friend. It is a most poisonous thing, and many of them are out there. We lost a boy last year." Damn, I thought. Steve wouldn't know a Caribbean yellowtail stingray if it bit him. Another half-hour passed.

Clayton pulled me aside. "Dude. We can get a chopper here in thirty minutes, but . . ." and he lowered his voice, "it's ten thousand dollars for a Coast Guard rescue." As a lawyer, I knew that cost was no object under these circumstances. "Hell, Clayton," I advised, "it's *Steve's* money!" So we agreed to make the call.

At that moment the Captain locked his searchlight on a body in the surf. It was Steve, dragging a fish behind him in the dark. Trolling for sharks, it seemed to me. When he made shore the rangers gave him and his fish a wide berth through the crowd. "Why are you blinding me with that light?" he asked. We told him about Ben's search and the rescue efforts, but he waved us off. "I know what I'm doing," he snapped, "and I don't need you guys to babysit me."

The captain listened nearby while the other rangers left to put the light and rescue gear away, shaking their heads. It was very late.

"*Bueno, muchacho,*" he said, his hand covering a smile.

Steve beamed proudly: "Yeah, at least we've got some good eating, right?" And he turned to take his catch away.

The captain turned to me.

"*Compadre,*" he grinned, "be careful near your friend's fish when he cleans it."

"Why?" I worried, "Is it bad to eat?"

"No, no, you can eat it," he assured me, "just don't touch it." My face showed that I didn't understand.

"Your friend," the captain explained, "has a Caribbean yellow-tail stingray on his line, and it just might kill him yet."

Needless to say, stingray was not our last meal on Isla Mona.

Last Run Down the Moose John

Welcome to Alaska, I thought, stumbling off the tarmac in Anchorage at midnight. My arms were full of bow tubes, my hands clasped tight through the gear bag straps that crossed my chest like bandoliers. The tubes were unsinkable, custom made for a two-week wilderness raft trip. The bags were bulging at their welded waterproof seams. It was too heavy, and I was too tired. Just the thought of more weight was a burden, but I stumbled to baggage claim for the rest. I wished I had packed light. In baggage, dogs and kids rode conveyors in and out of plastic-flap doors. Gold miners staked out the floor. Hippies and Inuits smoked while hunters pulled guns from bags, racked back the bolts and checked their sights. Yeah, welcome to big, wild, go-for-broke Alaska.

    I awoke with a jolt on my bags looking up at Jay Massey, the legend I had come to meet. He was tall and slim in his trademark plaid shirt, looking more like the newsman he used to be than the river guide he was. But he was a powerful writer whose raw, honest prose had drawn me to the Alaskan wilderness. I was there to raft the Moose John River, the trip Jay had pioneered. Still, I was in no hurry to launch. The man who literally wrote the book on Alaskan wilderness hunting was a captive source of knowledge, and I planned to absorb all I could. I had an appetite for Alaska.

We flew to McGrath, an outpost on the roadless edge of the wilderness. Pilots ran through the fuel-oiled air, holding their hats like soldiers in the air cavalry. Palettes of equipment swung under whumping propellers. Bush planes bustled in and out, including ours. I tossed my gear aboard and tried not to calculate the glide ratio of our groaning little workhorse. The pilot, Jay, my trip partner John Rice and our gear strained the single engine. We tracked a winding river toward the Moose John headwaters. Mountain slopes loomed above us. We were level with black bears on the foothills. Jay's lips moved, but I couldn't hear a word. "BLUEBERRIES!" His mouth moved again. "THE BEARS ARE ON THE BLUEBERRIES!" I still couldn't hear him, but I got the idea. It was great news. I had bear and moose tags.

There are no second takes, no safety nets for wilderness landings. Our pilot dove on a stony slope by the river that was impossibly short. Jay's near-fatal stall in *Bowhunting Alaska's Wild Rivers* worked its way into my head. On the first bounce I thought the odds may have been better taking it into the tree tops, wheels up. But I walked away, more or less intact, once I pried my hands free from the seat. The gravel bar was banked by the river on one side and raft frames and coolers on the other. We were the first of three groups, and would stay a few days to set up camp. In exchange, Jay would teach us rafting and bear and moose hunting technique before our two week stint on the river. Neither my partner nor I had been to Alaska before or rafted in the wilderness, let alone in the snow.

Bears surrounded base camp. The opportunities were as real as the dangers. Jay explained while he and I set up the tepee poles and skin: "Alaska's not a forgiving place," he said. "I know ten people who've been mauled by bears, and many more who died in bush planes. You have to decide for yourself what is acceptable risk." After that, the canvas walls seemed weak, but I slept hard despite the fear.

I woke with my face in drifting snow that blew in with the early pink light. Jay was asleep. John was up and gone. I rolled toward the stove and cinched the bag around me. If sleeping in was good enough for Jay Massey, it was good enough for me.

Jay's books on primitive archery and wilderness hunting were the reason I had come to Alaska. His adventures were larger than life. He was a "crusty old man" in his own words, but his hard line on hunting ethics seemed fresh as new snow to me. He had taken my calls and read my stories. I looked up to him, though he teased me mercilessly. "There's no governor on your psyche" he said, calling my Gore-Tex clothes and carbon longbow "as traditional as radar."

During the day Jay and I hunted when I wasn't learning to raft. Nights were warmed by debate and discussion, as he could be cantankerous. He didn't believe in compound bows, baiting bears, or Pope & Young. Still, while his opinions were forceful, they were always well thought out and articulate. I liked that. He spoke his mind without waiting to learn what you wanted to hear.

The five days passed too soon. In a freezing rain we inflated our rafts, bolted on rowing frames, and packed our gear. With a few last minute pictures, handshakes, and good words, we were ready to go. Jay pushed our rafts free. The last time I saw Jay Massey he was smiling in a cold rain on the Moose John, wearing his rain slicker, waving a hearty goodbye. He would be dead within a year.

Our warm tepee was sharp contrast to the river's biting cold. The Moose John is not a fast river, and difficult rapids are the exception. But pulling lines, oars, and rafts through icy water put a strain on our citified hands and backs. With eighty miles of river ahead of us, Alaska was already colder, wetter, and lonelier than anywhere I'd ever been.

Camp had been intensely quiet. Every small sound was amplified in the silence like a solo. In contrast, the river's white noise smothered every sound. It stole our hearing. But the landscape was brilliant and saturated with color and was compensation enough for deafness. We moved downriver as the graveled edges gave way to grasses, then alder bushes and beaver swamps. Beyond the swamps, mountains rose sharply on both sides of the water. Short, slippery lichens and berries covered the lower slopes. When the rain let up we saw black bears feeding just beneath the high country snow.

We bobbed on the water on rowing frames built onto the rafts. Gear was lashed to every strut or ring that would hold a rope. Bags, bow cases, and coolers were stuffed and stacked across my raft's bottom. Everything I had was in dry bags except my bow and arrows, which hung close on quick-release knots. I tried to waterproof myself in a knee-length hooded parka and hip boots, but freezing rain was a constant trial. I was raw, wet and cold.

Everything that came before was practice and preparation. Now we were in the Big Show. Each day was linked together by simple routines: making and breaking camp, planning and providing for our meals, hunting, trying to stay dry, calling for moose. Jay had tried to teach me the moose's wailing bellow but he'd finally given up and made me a mechanical call. It was a length of wet string pulled through a hole in a tin can, and the vibration made a dandy moosey moan. If it was traditional enough for Jay, it was traditional enough for me. We used it at every opportunity, always listening for an answer. Finally, we got one.

Calling from the rafts one afternoon, we swept around a bend into a bull moose who was expecting to meet a noisy lady coming downstream. He was knee-deep in water, head lowered in anticipation, peering out from under his wide, white rack. He seemed genuinely disappointed as we slowly floated by. When he walked off we came alive, paddling wildly against the current. John jumped out with his bow in hand and quickly caught the bull and two cows in a swamp.

For half an hour the moose guarded his cows. John was twenty yards away. It was an easy broadside shot. But as huge as the animal was, John was not sure its rack met the legal minimum. He tried all the estimating tricks Jay had shown us, but there was still doubt. Finally he backed away, unwilling to risk it. It was John's only real chance at a moose, and Jay would have been proud of his choice. I know I was.

As the days passed, salmon skeletons were piled higher on the banks, the mud trampled by grizzly and black bear tracks. The more fresh sign we found, the more anxious I was. I always wore my pistol, even on midnight potty breaks with my boots on and clothes off. I looked silly standing in my skivvies with a gun belt on, but I still took Jay's "guns on always" advice. When a black bear lumbered into camp after my chili, I was glad I did. I barely had time to unholster my gun and yell out while the bruin approached one very high-strung, shaky pistolero. John drew his gun, and even the bear sensed a shootout. He looked from me to the chili to John, thinking it over. Then he circled us for another run at the food. We turned with him, guns trained on every step. He finally backed away. It took both hands to get my shaking sidearm back in the holster. It would have been legal to take that bear with a pistol, but I never seriously considered it. As Jay had said, it was an *archery hunt*. After that, we strung tin cans around camp as a bear alarm.

The days wore on. Rafts sank, fingers froze, and everything leaked sooner or later. We fished grayling and salmon, hunted grouse, ate well, and chased bear and moose relentlessly. Day in and day out, we were reliably cold and wet, but we were still eager to hunt. We had many near chances at moose and black bear, but it was just not meant to be.

In the second week the weather turned unusually warm. Daytime temperatures blistered into the eighties. The hunting became predictably slow. Then we had our first human contact since we had left Jay. Breaking the solitude of the river, a native pilot buzzed us from the air repeatedly, driving game away from us toward his hunters. It was illegal, but unreportable under the circumstances. It made bowhunting impossible. After that we felt worn out and tired. With a long hunt behind us, we began the home stretch, a two-day row to our take-out.

The river branched into larger and slower runs until we washed out alone onto the mighty Kuskokwim. We were small specks on that big water. Cabins appeared and then settlements, and I began to worry that civilization, when I reached it, might swallow me whole like the Kuskokwim swallowed the Moose John. I had been alone and at peace on that river, in a way I had never known in the city. I didn't want to lose that feeling.

Jay said we would know our take-out by the sound of generators powering the settlement. A low rumble announced Stoney River like some self-contained outpost after Armageddon. As we pulled to the docks our smell alarmed the sled dogs. Every team in Stoney River howled our arrival, drowning out the generators. We stepped ashore on wobbly legs after sixteen good days on the water, and started the long journey home.

Jay and I spoke often after the trip, making plans for future books and hunts. He was writing a third novel and hoped to find a publisher. Then one night he called late to ask about cancer. There was nothing I could tell him he didn't already know. In a few short months he passed on. He left behind his wife and little girl, Martha and Sophia, and thousands of admirers of his writing and his life. I am one of them.

I still dream sometimes about the roar of the water in my ears, and the slap and splash of oars on the raft. I sometimes feel the raft's rocking motion as I sleep, and remember the big, hard country high above the water. And I always remember the feeling of being alone and at peace, on the river Jay Massey named.

Jay Massey glassing on cliffs above the Moose John River.

Longbow

Molokai Madness

"Walter Naki's your man, but you'd better be in shape."
"You going with Walter?—better be in shape."
"Oh yeah, I can take you, but you better be in shape.
... How old are you?"

I agreed to give a lecture in Oahu, but it wasn't Oahu I wanted to see. It was her lonely little sister Molokai. Molokai, with her lush cliffs and misty valleys, wild deer, goats, and pigs. Walter Naki agreed to show me his little Hawaiian jewel, but he said it was a tough hunt. I didn't listen. I was mad for Molokai, infatuated, too hot for the trip to pay attention. I ignored his warnings and looked past the heat and elevation. I slipped his questions about my fitness like a boxer on the ropes. I barged in, leading with my chin, until Molokai hit me like an asphalt mop. She nearly killed me.

There wasn't time to plan, or get in shape. Jack Harrison overnighted a take-down Black Wolf longbow to test on the island. It shot well and fast and it fit as luggage on the four leg flight from Tampa. But that was the extent of my preparation. I was badly out of shape. Only a week after I spoke to Walter I landed on Oahu, gave my speech, suffered through a luau, threw off my leis, and raced to my date with Molokai at dawn.

On Molokai the jungle meets the sea at the mouth of Halawa Valley, near the trailhead at Moalua falls. Walter drove without lights on rough beach roads, bouncing coffee into my lap and sweet rolls to the floor. We lurched to a stop in the sand, covered by the white noise of water pounding rocks in the dark. I couldn't see, but I could smell the salt. The waterfall mists into the pool, then runs over rocks to the Pacific past rough driftwood shacks. Fishermen there claim the beach by possession, not title, and guard it from outsiders. Walter walked me past their hostile stares, and I was glad for the safe passage. We began to get vertical, climbing from sea level toward the top of Molokai's nearly 5,000 foot peaks.

In an hour's climb I had to rest. Not a good sign. Maui shimmered nearby under a blistering sunrise. The sun climbed and dragged the jungle heat and humidity with it. Whales jumped below, but I could only think about their cool ocean spray. I was sweating and overheated and had barely begun. I was becoming dehydrated. I realized I was not only out of shape, I was stupid. Walter told me to take more water but I only packed two liters, which had always been enough for one day. Worse, for the first time in years I left my water filter and iodine tablets behind to save space in my pack.

By eight o'clock my water was gone. I had two choices: drink ground water or turn back. Mountain water once gave me amoebic dysentery and a two-week hospital stay, but I wasn't going to quit this trip. I would drink water where we found it, despite the risk of dysentery. I would take the chance.

We climbed on goat trails, chasing sign. My legs were shaky, but I looked past the pain to the hunt. We had glimpses of goats and pigs, but in stands of Guava and Pele grass too tight to hunt. The game is drawn to guava, but the fruit wasn't ripe. We climbed higher. When we reached the top, the jungle gave way to open fields. "Plane Crash" was named for the World War Two fighter still crumpled in the bush. We could see Hipuapua Falls and below it the leper colony of Kalaupapa, dating to the 1800s. On the ocean near Umilehi point, below the highest sea cliffs in the world, Hawaii exiled its lepers with the most beautiful view in the islands. The disease has been treatable since WWII, but over eighty lepers still live at the colony, too old or tired to leave. Old and tired was just how I felt. Walter slowed down to let me breathe, but I was soaked through my clothes. I left a sweat trail in the dust behind me.

There were fresh tracks and droppings, and a panoramic view of the islands. We sat to eat, rest, and glass down the steep sloping valleys. I needed the breather. I took my boots off to inspect my blisters, and drank the pond water I had filtered through a scarf. Walter told me of a client taking five animals in a day, but my mind was more on getting home than taking trophies. As he talked and I patched my bloody feet, three axis bucks grazed into view on a distant hill, maybe a quarter mile as the crow flies, but impossible for me given the vertical challenges. The largest was 150 pounds or so, with trophy horns. I turned down the chance, and Walter was disappointed. I felt bad for both of us. In another hour three big hogs crashed out of the brush and bedded down two hundred yards away. My legs were stiff, but the pigs seemed close enough to try.

I slipped down the slope into a streambed that hid me from sight. But my legs trembled with any real strain. Vines caught my feet. I stumbled over rocks. I fell twice, a sure sign of exhaustion. I pushed on. One hundred and fifty yards later I struggled up the bank to look, but . . . no pigs. Walter pointed them out from a distance, and I crawled off. Crawling was easier than walking. Tall grass moved above rooting pigs thirty yards away. They came into full view, but there was no cover to hide me. I drew on the closest black boar from my knees. He bolted, but then stopped uphill to stare at me. Walter thinks they don't know what people are, and are curious. I had time to aim. I even accounted for the slope. But at forty yards I didn't account for the flat trajectory of the new Black Wolf bow, and the arrow sailed high. I was disappointed. I had come so far and missed so badly, but missing was not my greatest concern. I took a handful of Advil, drank my brown warm water, and told my guide I was done.

Walter wanted to find me another chance. I wanted to avoid a helicopter rescue. An hour downhill, my legs shook and I felt sick. I threw up into the bushes. My head was pounding. My feet were shredded. We stopped in the shade of guava trees where I lay on my back until the world stopped spinning. I was beside a cool stream in an open grove and felt that I might never move again. While I rested, Walter blew a grunt tube to mimick the social sounds of pigs. I lifted my head. If I couldn't go to the pigs, Walter could bring the pigs to me. I didn't know it was possible. He asked if I had the strength to shoot. I came to my knees and raised my bow. A young boar rustled out of the grass and I sent an arrow through him. Another came to the commotion and a second shoat fell for the barbecue. They were only runts, the size to roast whole, but Walter had to pack them both. I had nothing left.

Hours of downhill hiking in the sun lay ahead. The only water was in pig wallows, but I drank it. I put one limping foot in front of the other. I took more Advil. I dreamed about the iced drinks in Walter's truck. Three hours later we broke out of the jungle under the waterfall. I stood in the cool falling spray, drinking Gatorade from Walter's cooler. I threw it up in the bushes, then drank more and was sick again. I stood in the water a long time, feeling I would never cool off.

In nine hours we covered ten miles and four thousand feet

of elevation. We saw eleven deer, two goats, nine pigs, and five humpback whales. My feet were blistered, bloody and raw. I was dizzy and hot and my muscles ached. I could almost feel Giardia working its way through my intestines. I was sick. I was mad from Molokai. When Walter dropped me off at the airport I could barely look at him. I changed my clothes, bandaged my feet, and boarded Air Molokai for home, a twenty-four hour trip. I promised to return for my pride but I never did. Molokai had floored me in the first round, and one round of Molokai Madness was enough.

Longbow

Last Trip with the Old Man

My dad died this fall. Not suddenly or peacefully, but at least in the arms of my mother and me, knowing we loved him. His body had turned on him from the inside and sucked the life out until there was barely enough skin to cover his bones. He held me tight as he let go of his life and then he was gone. Late that night, when the officers and funeral directors and well-wishers had gone, my family finally slept. I sat awake.

I am a hunter, an archer, and a man of the outdoors, but I live in the city, far from my friends afield. I sat awake, wanting to talk to someone who might understand my pain and my plans. Alone at home, I turned to something different from the campfire, the church, or even the local bar—the internet.

On a message board for traditional archers, I wrote on my computer, broadcasting to anyone out there listening:

> *My dad died today, and I have a family uncertain about the best way to recognize the meaning of a man's life, and the best way to bring closure to his life and death for adults and children alike.*

Longbow

But it came to me that not long ago we shared a campsite in the Colorado Flattops—Dad, Mom, my wife and our four kids. A July camp that was at such an altitude and weather we lost a packhorse on the string to the cold overnight. I still remember Dad waking me up at 4:00 am to plan a way to break the news to the kids gently, they were so attached to the horses by then.

I've returned there since in the fall, longbow in hand, for the elk and grouse that always escape me, and marveled at the beauty of the plain at eleven thousand feet—the flowers, grasses, trees (and that aging horse's bones). So it suddenly came to me today, and I've decided. Next week I'll drag my tired and now very old body back up to "Dead Horse Flat" with Dad's cremated remains, and float them from the head of a rock spring through a small stream that feeds the whole hilltop plain.

And in years to come, my kids and I will have a place to go (although it's no easy trip) where Grandpa has nourished and become the things he loved while he was there, and where we can remember a good time and a final resting place for the old man (and the horse he rode in on).

If only the FDA, CDC, and Funeral Directors Association don't find out, I should be OK. And down the road, maybe Dad, as a tasty morsel of grass, can bring an elk within my limited range. I sure haven't been doing so well myself, and I could use his help.

Remember to hold 'em close while they're here. They're too soon gone, and too far away to reach once they go.

Despite the lateness of the day, within minutes and hours I began to receive an outpouring of support and kind feeling, all from people I had never met in person. All were gracious, insightful, and kind, and assured me that the plan for my father's last journey was sound:

Last Trip with the Old Man

Jay, you still have your Dad. He'll be there in the mirror every morning, and in your children's laughter and dancing eyes. My family's thoughts and good wishes are with you. - Jim

A beautiful eulogy Jay. Forget the FDA and the funeral guys. Put your dad where he belongs—on top of that mountain. - Lee

My condolences to you Jay for your loss today . . . Interesting way to describe your intentions for your father's last rites. I mentioned a similar scenario to my wife recently, whenever that day comes for me, but she has no conception of why I would wish such a thing. I guess only those in kindred spirit can truly understand such things. May you find peace at this time of loss. Best of luck to you. - Doug

Condolences on your father's passing. I think we owe a debt to our loved ones that goes beyond what the funeral directors require. I did almost the same thing with my wife's cremated remains, which was her express wish. They lie on a high ridge overlooking a cold creek in a place far more peaceful than any cemetery I've ever seen. - Gene

Jay, sorry to hear about your loss. Words at a time like this always seem to fall short of expressing one's true emotion, but your words sure painted a picture of a son that truly loves his father. Your dad will like his new home in the mountains. A fitting resting place for a man of the outdoors if there ever was one. I'll keep the Campbell family in my prayers tonight. - Chuck

Congratulations to your father. Job well done. Up to you now. - JK

It *was* up to me. I arranged my pack and, within a few days, set off with my father's remains to beat the high country snow. By plane, car, and horseback, I traveled from Tampa to a trailhead in the Colorado Flattop Mountains, then set off on foot to "Dead Horse Flat." I took my bow and arrows along (I hoped Dad would want us to hunt on our last trip), and spent six days alone at eleven thousand feet, thinking, hiking, hunting, and writing. The weather was strikingly, uncommonly beautiful, sunny and bright in October.

When it came time to part with my dad, I had the ceremony, brief and sparsely attended as it was, that let me lay a great weight down and leave it on that mountain. It was more important to me than anything I've done yet in this life. I recorded it in my journal later that day:

> *Well there, I've done it. Up at 5:00 am, on the trail by 6:00, up on top before 8:00. Found our old family campsite and the bones of that poor dead horse. Found the head of that rock spring. Spread Dad's ashes right in the water flowing down to the lake. It's a pretty spot—you can see the stream and lake from there. Left some ashes in a small mound on a rock in the spring—the wind and rain will spread them.*
>
> *Said a eulogy—some words—the one from JK was the best I've heard. I couldn't do better. "Congratulations old man. Job well done. It's up to me now. I love you. I'll miss you." Fired one arrow into the sun—told him I'll be back.*
>
> *More ceremony than he wanted, I guess, but it was just the two of us. Remembered the kids playing here, riding "their" horses, and sliding down the hills in the snow in July. Came back down.*

A strange thing happened. Every day afterward, I climbed and bugled for elk for miles without any sign of one. But on my last day I hiked back up to the spring for a final word with the old man. And while I was sitting there by the cold water, talking to myself, an elk bugled so close behind it made me jump. As I turned my head, I glimpsed the elk's buckskin back slipping into the dark timber. I said goodbye to my father, and stood up to give chase.

Thanks, Pop. See you next year.

My father, Reid Campbell, the Old Man. Here he was in flight training in WWII. A P-47 Thunderbolt pilot, he was shot down twice, escaped once although badly burned, and spent time in a German prison camp before Patton freed his camp. His family had been notified he was lost in action.

Longbow

THE CLOSET

I went through my father's things last year, through his closet with the piles of stuff he meant to sort and catalog and arrange before he died but never did. I expected to find the old man's story in those boxes and papers, but I found mine instead — my young life recorded in school reports and letters and drawings. In the back corner of the closet, behind the old suits and boxes and bent brown shoes, leaned a soft shotgun case, its long, dusty narrow end folded down over something much smaller than the case was meant to hold. I knew that case, and what was in it, and the memory made my collar tight. I wished Pop had buried the damn thing thirty years ago like he said he would.

I was ten when I first saw that soft gun case under the tree. It was Christmas, the best Christmas ever. It must have been on sale for Pop to buy that old mismatched case, or maybe they tossed it in with the deal to get rid of it. It was nearly twice as long as the rifle inside and folded over the barrel of the gun like an old limp sock. But it didn't matter—Pop had bought me a rifle after all! A Remington Nylon 66 .22 rifle. Man, that was the one I wanted. It wasn't one of those old-timey wooden-stock long guns but a short, space-age trapper's rifle I could carry anywhere on the farm, even on horseback. I spent most of my time out there alone anyway, out in the deep woods around our farm, and with that gun I could finally hunt. Hunting was something we could share, the other farm creatures and me.

The best hunters were the cats, my barn cats. Bru, the old mother cat, could sit like a stone through the morning, waiting for a trespassing rabbit or rodent to move. I often sat by my kitchen window, watching for her twitching ear or some rustling grass to give away the target. Then she would spring up from the weeds, a furious ball of twisting, heartless, hot-blooded predator, taking on rabbits twice her size to feed her litters. Sometimes I marched back to the barn with her and sat nearby on the hay bales watching the kittens eat. She was my after-school companion, shadowing me on my walks, hunting out in the fields beside me. I loved that cat.

With the gun I became a hunter too. Bru had her rabbits, but groundhogs were my passion. As a bonus Pop gave me a bounty of fifty cents for every dead groundhog. Fifty cents! I was rich. That gun became like a part of my arm, and I could hit anything. I shot it for any reason, all of the time. My judgment wasn't always good, as Pop learned when he traced the new leaks in his barn roof to my pigeon extermination program. I lost the gun for a while over that, but I did my time like a man and finally got it back in exchange for a promise to shoot straight.

With pigeons off my target list, the dim-witted groundhogs quickly became scarce. I turned to long-range shooting. The open sights were a challenge but I focused on the bounty and became a better shot. In time I was taking the beasts at seventy-five, then one hundred yards. But the remaining rodents were wary. I learned to hunt like Bru, waiting behind brush piles, holding dead still until a groundhog sat up near a distant mound of dirt. I learned to rest my light rifle on dirt piles, and breathe easy on the trigger pull. I learned to be patient, like my feral mother cat.

The groundhogs thinned out and money got tight. The bounty barely bought the bullets anymore. I was desperate for money. I spent my weekends in the field looking for longer-range, harder targets. I remember working to get in position one afternoon, with the shadows long and the shooting light low. I remember how much I wanted the cash. I remember seeing a groundhog's head, still like a stone near a rock pile a hundred yards away. I rested the rifle on a mound of dirt and aimed low into the weeds where the body was a bigger target. I remember how sure I was of the shot, such a long shot, with only open sights.

I remembered all that then, although I had buried it for thirty years until I saw the case again. When I pulled the trigger there was a whistling moment before the bullet hit, a perfect shot. Then she sprang up from the weeds, a furious ball of twisting, hopeless, bloody cat. My cat. I dropped the rifle and I ran and held her. Then I ran home to my mother with Bru and I both covered in blood, only one of us shot.

The vet eased the body away from me, and left me and my mother in the waiting room. Mom took my arm to lead me home and started to say something. It seemed hard for her to find the right word. "Defecation," she finally said, stumbling past the cruder term for what she meant. I was covered in "defecation," and we had to go home and clean me up. I didn't know what the word meant then, but I got the idea. She was right. I was covered in it, and no bath would ever make me clean again. For thirty years I had kept that old memory at bay, until I saw the misfit gun case folded over in the closet.

I still don't know why Pop kept that old gun all those years. He should have thrown it out like he said he would. I should have thrown it out too, but I didn't. I brought it from his home to mine and put it away, out of sight, behind my old suits and boxes and bent brown shoes. Back in the corner, with its long dusty narrow end folded over the barrel like a limp sock.

Back in the closet.

Back in the Black Water

I went to the swamp again in May, wading through the black water and water moccasins, carrying my longbow, chasing pigs. An open tarp roped on an oak island was my camp, and gave me shade. I was glad to be in the Florida woods again. The oak ceilings and grey moss curtains are as comfortable as a parlor, if you're willing to entertain the alligators.

The full moon rose before the sun fell, and the twin globes hung on the horizon like the two moons of Mars. But my thoughts were not on the cosmos. I waded in a string of black water to cover my scent and sound. I stopped and listened, facing the wind. When a clearing opened to the bank I climbed up and sat in the wet grass near its edge. The swamp smells stronger and the mosquitoes swarm thicker on the ground, but my senses are sharper sitting low and still.

As the shadows stirred, a curious grunt sounded in the thick scrub. I grunted back. I hoped to tease the pig into my clearing and get position for a shot. Instead it ran to me, scattering leaves and cracking palmettos. There was nowhere to hide. I dropped flat on my face in the watery grass and the mud soaked me through. Ten steps away, a boar broke into the clearing. I was looking up at him. He seemed big as a cow.

He shook his black muddy mane and swung his head from side to side. He grunted and looked for whatever had made the noise. I was still flat in the weeds, but when he turned away I took a chance. I rose up on both knees with the bow level to the ground and released. The arrow clipped the tips of the grass on the way to his chest. When the broadhead struck he bucked in a whirl of mud and grunts and tore back into the thick oak scrub. I jumped up to chase him. He didn't stop. Neither did I.

I ran in the clearing alongside the snap and crack of branches breaking in the cover. The sun slipped below the treeline. The pig stopped running and lay down. I knelt to listen, but with night coming I crawled close, straining, finally catching a patch of hair through the

A backlit Florida pig spots the author in a central Florida swamp.

bushes. I drew an arrow to my cheek and released it at the black swatch. Again the bushes blew up and again I followed the explosion, chasing flashes of black in the fading light. When the branches stopped breaking we both collapsed. I could see his eyes in the thicket, staring back at mine.

I was out of breath. My chest hurt. I nocked a third arrow, waiting for him to run away. He ran, but this time the bushes broke in my direction. Black hair flashed through the branches. I was frozen. There was nowhere to hide. He cleared the palmettos six steps away on a dead run, trailing blood, his eyes on mine again. I drew the bow more to fend him off than to shoot. I released a third time and jumped free. The steel head buried in his shoulder, and the pig turned back to the oaks. My quiver was empty.

I stood in the open outside the hammock. The best plan was to return to camp and wait. I backtracked on my trail instead, hoping an arrow might have come free in the bush. Thirty yards away I found my first shaft buried in the ground where it had passed through the pig. I pulled it free and cleaned the feathers. I returned to the palmettos. The hammock was quiet. I turned on a headlight and took up the trail.

I twisted through the brambles slowly, finding licks of blood on a game trail. It opened up, making walking easier. Then I saw him on the trail, facing me. I drew for the fourth time, but eased the arrow down. He had been waiting for me, but I arrived too late. He died in place, my last arrow through his chest, anchored in the sand. I sat down.

The smell of pig was strong, the mosquitoes thick around him. The mud soaked through my jeans but I didn't care. The swamp came alive again with the nervous sounds of frogs and bugs quieted by the ruckus. I gathered my breath and my thoughts.

When I was young, books about hunting with the bow inspired me to pick up a weapon even Native Americans had abandoned.

Fred Bear and Howard Hill were well known then. It was a different time when adventurous hunters could be heroes. In my boyhood fantasies I had been the master of the longbow and the cedar shaft. Rabbits on my farm became dangerous game charging my arrows. But as I grew I put the bow away and with it thoughts of Hill and Bear and their adventures in the wild.

Until then. Thirty years after those boyhood hunts I sat muddy and wet in the swamp and the dark and I remembered those dreams once again. Shouldering my bow and my last salvaged arrow, I stood up and started back for camp.

I ran all the way.

The End of the Northern Road

Today the trip to the Arctic Ocean is only inconvenient. The journey doesn't sift through pilgrims anymore, leaving the weak dead and bundled behind on the trail. Still, few folks make their way to the end of the northern road these days. That makes it better for those of us who finally pull the dream of Alaska off the shelf and go. The Alaskan tundra, that boggy twelve inches of peat covering the treeless arctic permafrost, is a mostly unspoiled wilderness.

In northern Alaska an archery hunting zone, a summer season, and caribou herds all intersect on the Dalton Highway, also known as the Haul Road. It runs from Fairbanks to Prudhoe Bay, following the Alaska pipeline to the Arctic Ocean. It cuts through resident caribou herds for hundreds of miles, and the land is reserved for five miles on either side for archers.

North of the Brooks mountain range, the highway and the pipeline follow the Sagavanirktok River, known as the Sag. Along the Sag, fishing for grayling and hunting for ptarmigan fill the endless summer days. Black and grizzly bears, rabbit and even muskoxen wander with the caribou, and the dinner plate stays full if the weather allows.

But weather is an angry companion on the Haul Road, with violent mood swings.

Alaskans say there are two kinds of people who go to Alaska: those who want to and those who have to. The Reverend Scotty Bennett drank himself north twenty-two years ago. He had to go. But today his hands are steady as he builds houses for the homeless. He is a minister to men too troubled to cope, men who are like he once was, who have come to the end of the road. With his full beard and thick spectacles, he looks more like a prospector than a minister, a look that suits him best when he guides hunters in the fall.

When Scotty invited me to bowhunt the Dalton in August, he suggested that I should prepare for sun, wind, rain, snow, and ice. I heeded his good words, and packed for extremes, with heavy wool, fleece, and Gore-Tex. Most good advice goes unused, but I wrung every benefit out of that heavy gear, and I did it all in what passes for summer up north.

I flew from Tampa to Fairbanks in August, as hard-driven snow blanketed everything north to Prudhoe Bay. We had to pull the wipers on Scotty's old Toyota truck by hand, as the Reverend's prayers to a greater power couldn't soften the storm. It was not the endless summer I had left behind in Florida. Seventy-five miles from the Arctic Ocean, we set our tents against the blow and hunkered down, moving only to patch leaks and replace stakes. Snow overloaded our shelters. For most of four days we hibernated while our four-season shelters luffed and snapped in the forty-knot blow. Temperatures never rose above the thirties. Welcome, Alaska said, to August in the Brooks Range. At least the bugs were manageable.

The fourth day the weather blew off, leaving us buried in snow. Scotty's truck sported a flat tire. We spent a day on repairs in Prudhoe Bay, but we had it soft. Nearby Barrow had been evacuated during the worst August storm in twenty years. Alaska gives you just what it wants you to have, which is usually more, and sometimes very much more, than you expected. We settled in back at camp under clear skies, with one day left to hunt.

In the morning my tent glowed hot under the new sun and forced me out into the snowmelt. Scotty was ready with coffee in the good weather, just as he had been in the bad, when he would cheerfully lie about our chances for the sun to shine. He had built up a substantial account of good Karma, and as the weather and our fortunes shifted to the good, he was most deserving of the benefit that came his way.

While Scotty and I dried our damaged gear, a pair of young hunters drove into camp with coolers of fresh salmon and caribou steaks, and asked us to celebrate surviving the storm. Billy Lewis had the look of a modern Viking, redheaded and energetic. His hunting partner, Benji Hill, was tall and filled out his coat like a weightlifter. They'd driven up from Montana a month before, and filled their coolers with salmon and caribou before the storm. They were dishing out companionship, conversation, and tailgate cuisine. They carried wooden bows and feathered arrows, and knew an old school archery camp when they saw one.

We soon warmed our faces over steaming plates of pepper-grilled salmon steaks and fresh, butter-seared caribou loins. We sat elbow to elbow on the ground, an overturned canoe at our back. The snow-packed Brooks Range wrapped the horizon. The Sag river ran to our left, and a spur of low, rolling hills rose on our right. The whole of Alaska was our dinner theatre. We were grateful for the food and sun and ate quietly, gazing along the river. A wobbly pair of sticks on the horizon became a set of bobbing antlers. We kept eating. The caribou bull kept coming.

Except to raise a fork, no one moved until the bull had nearly closed the distance. It was hard to quit those salmon steaks. Scotty finally slapped his plate down and stood up, exasperated, as if *someone* had to do the dirty job. He refused to trade his coveralls for camouflage. "Boys, dressed like this I'll scare that bull quick and be back for my slice of pie. Keep it warm for me!" The bull ambled away up the rolling hills to our right, taking no notice of camp. Scotty matched him stride for easy stride, staying a hundred yards back and downwind. Only a few minutes after the Reverend crested the hill, he rose again, the sun's rays streaming out around him. He raised both arms high, and called out the good news. Scotty had taken his first caribou with the tools of the ancients. What a show.

He couldn't stop talking when we reached him. "That little bull wandered around up here like a tumbleweed in a whirlywind," he jabbered. "He finally parked his head under a willow bush no bigger than his antlers and lay down. He was just a teenager; he didn't know no better. Jay, I'm gonna hunt in these overalls and sneakers all the time. It's Prudhoe Bay camo—I look like a *pipeline* man!"

He had forgotten his pie, which was good since we'd already eaten it. He kept talking:

"Those big hickory shafts will knock the hop out of a rabbit, but they're so dang slow and heavy I had to get close enough to lob one in there." He kicked at the bulky clumps of grass around our feet. "Oh man, these tussocks are hard to stalk on—I felt like a drunk walking on a field of basketballs."

He was right about the tundra. Packing his caribou back to camp I fell in wet holes between the big balls of sod more than once. But Scotty kept talking as I watched for bears that might have winded his caribou. I always watched for bears.

"I scooted in close and squatted down behind that bush and let one fly. That big arrow drew in like a guided missile. It spun into his ribs, then disappeared right through him."

The young caribou had died in place. The three of us set down frames, knives, and game bags, posted guard, and worked as a team with Scotty to quarter and haul the meat before brown bears found the kill. It was quick work. Every muscle came off the animal before the antlers, which we brought down with the hide in the last load. It was good meat that would take care of the Reverend's homeless flock through the winter. With the game bags tied up high, we were tired, full and happy, and we slept soundly, dreaming of clear days on the Dalton.

Reverend Scotty Bennett and his first caribou taken with a bow on the Haul Road, just south of Prudhoe Bay, Alaska.

Longbow

Finding Will

Will Cooley had been lost, presumed dead, APB'd and abandoned, found, resurrected, banished for life, then welcomed back and forgiven, all on one Super Bowl night. That's a lot of work for any man on a night when most of America is in a football coma. It was probably harder for Will himself, who was said to be a middle-aged fat man with a heart condition. I wouldn't know, because I never really saw him, no more than I might have seen a ghost.

I had no business in a Georgia swamp during a January ice storm, but an invitation to hunt with my longbow is always difficult to resist. As it happened, I'd been asked to fill in at the last minute for a celebrity hunter who knew enough to read a weather report. But I'm not as smart as a celebrity hunter, nor as choosy. I got the invitation on Sunday night and Monday morning I was sliding toward Savannah in an ice storm.

I should have turned back, but I was headed to Milton, a magazine-cover private Mecca for hunters. It was rumored that famous archery pioneers Maurice and Will Thompson had hunted the Milton land a century before, though I never saw evidence of them. I was tired of the public land hunting that was available to me, so when Milton's owner Broderick Stoddard picked me as a last-minute substitution, I packed without a second thought. Those would come later.

Close to Savannah fresh sleet hardened on the wipers. It was already a record-breaking cold, and the temperature dropped further as the afternoon faded. But when I pulled up, everyone who was coming was ready to hunt. Except for Will, Broderick Stoddard's close friend, who had not shown up.

The first hand to take mine was attached to Andy Sanderson, a surgeon and near blood kin to Stoddard (who wasn't expected to make it down this trip). Like Stoddard, Andy was a man of God, powerfully committed to passing along the Word. Bald under his fedora, tall, bookish and bright-looking in glasses, he wore his good humor as openly as his faith. Given Stoddard and Andy's influence, this was not a camp in which one could casually curse, and I always felt an apology coming on, if only for what I might do or say later.

On the other hand, bowyer Danny Borders was the devil's own balance to Andy and Stoddard's reverence. A self-confessed curmudgeon, Danny kept those boys simultaneously on their toes and off-balance when talking about faith, but always with impish humor. Then there was Jimmy. A friend to Danny and an author in his own right, he was happy to absorb Danny's barbs and benevolence, packaged in some private arrangement between them. He was a steady younger man to be counted on.

Stoddard was the elephant in the room. Despite his absence, he was always present as our benefactor. He was reported to be down to earth and easygoing, a construction man interested in anything to do with land, especially hunting. Andy pulled his coat tight, and looked up through snow that was blowing thick. "Let's hunt, boys. This storm is rolling in like a freight train."

We set out in trucks and parked close to the edge of a hunting paradise. Milton's five-thousand acres of high pine, oak bottom, and swampland were only hunted by Stoddard's private guests a few times a year. The ponds were full of alligators, world-class bass, and crappie. It being January, we were there to hunt pigs. And pigs being pigs, we expected to find them out and about, nevermind the ice and snow. It didn't quite work out that way.

I slipped through the wet and ice alone, and the only pig I found was a small shoat. But I was hunting with stone arrowheads, and a barbecue-sized shoat was as good a test for the hand-knapped head as a bruiser hog. I took the shot, but the pig took my arrow with him into the water of the thick Georgia swamp. I lost him, and returned to the main road, feeling bad about the pig.

Jimmy met me at his truck at dusk.

"Any luck?"

"Only bad. Hit a shoat, lost my arrow."

"Hey, that Ford wasn't here when we came in, was it?"

We wondered together whose car was parked on the roadside. Whoever it belonged to, he had come in after us. Back at camp, Andy was also puzzled. We drove out again to see who was on the private lease—the acreage was locked up pretty tight. In the headlights' glare, Andy identified it as Will's car. Will was a friend of Stoddard's with full hunting privileges. Andy didn't seem concerned.

"He'll find his way back to camp soon enough. That's what he does. He'll stop for a cup of coffee before he goes home."

No worries. Again we returned to camp. But as the rain fell and the ice thickened on the ground and still there was no Will, we became worried. Every few minutes someone would step out onto the porch, stub a toe at the thickening crust of ice, and look off in the direction of the swamp.

Most people are optimists and hold off on jumping to hard conclusions. Not me. I'm a pessimist. I figure that when one door closes, another one slams shut. When Will didn't come in on time, I started thinking the worst. It comes from having been a cop, a fireman, and a lawyer. Andy and my campmates did not share my gloom at first, but by eight we were collectively concerned about Will's fate. It was time to start searching.

We began with reasonable, neighborly efforts to drive the roads, assuming Will would turn up in the headlights, trudging back to his car. But Jimmy found a dead pig on the roadside, a big boar, its side cut with Will's distinctive four-blade broadhead. Footprints in the mud and snow indicated Will had dragged the pig out of the swamp late and then headed back in. That just didn't make any sense. A couple of us set out a quick grid search. Darned if we didn't find a dead sow in the swamp fifty yards into the black water, dragged up on a log out of the wet. Same four-blade strike. Dang. And a few yards further in, another blood trail led into the cold, dark water. Three pigs?

But no Will. Now it was ten, truly late, and the group was becoming frantic. Andy said that Will never hunted with a pack or gear, not even a good coat. And Andy, as a doctor and Will's friend, knew that Will had a bad heart.

"I don't see how he could have hauled two pigs in this cold, bad as his heart is." Andy seemed sure that the stress of dragging two or three pigs out of the swamp had killed his friend. He began to speak of Will's death as a foregone conclusion. I assumed that for Andy to be so sure that Will had passed, Will's heart must have been a sticky mess long before he waded into that swamp.

Andy called Stoddard, who got in his car up in Atlanta and started driving south through the storm. And Stoddard, a wealthy man who knew how to get action when he needed it, called the local sheriff, who in turn called out a search party of trucks, men, and dogs. All hell was about to break loose.

We were still performing grid searches when a wagon train of official trucks and four wheelers spun up through the rutted back roads of Milton. Steam rose from the heat of the engines, lights bounced through the low-lying exhaust fumes, cigarette and cigar smoke wafted up, generators rumbled, and tracking hounds howled with their heads out of windows as their handlers yelled at them to quiet down.

When professionals arrive to push out well-meaning amateurs, there's bound to be a little tension, especially if the professionals blame the amateurs for ruining the dogs' scent trail by stomping all over it. Andy jimmied open Will's car and got a shirt for the dogs to use for scent, but the hounds just went in circles, usually coming back to the dead pigs for a snoot full of blood and bristles. Those dogs, not being A-Team hounds from a big-city department like Atlanta, found dead pigs much more interesting than the man they had been brought in to track. After watching a few rounds of circling, howling, pig-snuffling dog work, Stoddard stepped in and demanded that the sheriff bring in a heat-seeking helicopter, ice storm be danged. He might have said something unkind to the sheriff about the hounds, but if he did it got lost in the barking and engine noise. In the south, however, it's best to speak kindly about a man's dogs and his truck if you want to get along.

In any event, that conversation brought an end to the professional phase of the search for Will Cooley.

"Mr. Stoddard," the sheriff said, chewing the end of a big cigar and spitting through the headlights, "your man is dead or alive, one or the other, and he'll likely be the same in the morning." He spat again for effect, and had the rapt attention of the hounds. "That's when we'll be back."

He circled a finger in the air as if he was pulling those trucks and men into a line with his one pudgy digit. They all horsed up and left as fast as they had come, smoke trailing, hounds howling out the windows, splattering mud and ice behind them. But we still didn't have Will. We were left alone in the cold and dark, and felt lost ourselves as we drove back to the camp house. I could feel then what was coming, and I wished that I had gone home with the bloodhounds to get some sleep.

It was 2:00 am at this point, and "exhausted" didn't cover my weariness. But Stoddard wasn't about to let us abandon Will in the swamp, dead or alive. Stoddard and Andy had called Will's wife, who could only sit awake crying by the phone as the roads were now closed in the storm. Will, Stoddard, and Andy were close friends, and Stoddard and Andy were clearly feeling guilty. Guilty, I suppose, for not insisting that Will take a phone or a pack or even a heavy jacket when hunting on Stoddard's property. Like the guilt your mother felt for not dressing you warm enough when you came home with a cold, but so much worse. As Will's friends they felt the loss differently than Danny, Jimmy, and I. Danny had nodded off while Stoddard decided what to do, but as newcomers, Jimmy and I didn't carry the seniority for sleep. We were gently ushered out the door to continue the search, blessed by Stoddard to the powers that be. Of course, the powers that be weren't going back out in the slush storm with us at two in the morning. As much as Jimmy and I wanted to go to bed, we didn't feel welcome back in camp without Will. We were looking for him with impure motives, I suppose, which makes it ironic that we were rewarded almost instantly. Rather than treading the same black water, Jimmy and I started guessing. Not the "what would I have done if I was Will" kind of guessing, but the "Naw, Will couldn't have done that" kind of guessing. The kind that makes you look for something where it just couldn't be, the way you finally discover a set of lost keys or your two year old.

On an unfounded hunch, we drove a mile away from where Will just *had* to be, far from the deep swamp and down into a pine draw. For Will to be there, he would have had to wade a few hundred yards through waist deep water in the pitch black, in the worst winter storm in a decade. There was no chance he was down there. But we got out of the truck and honked and hollered anyway, and whistled and shouted, and generally made so much noise that we went deaf for a moment in the night. Then we heard something. Maybe.

People have the sense that noise carries well in the outdoors, but it doesn't. Trees, wind, snow, and hills rob sound of its initiative and leave it alone in the wild. Just like Will. But something deep in the woods had pushed enough air our way to brush our eardrums. We both felt it. It had direction, if nothing else. So we kicked through the understory, chasing that little push of air through the palmettos until it finally turned into . . . Will.

It was so dark and sleeting we never really saw Will even when he was standing in front of us. We just heard his voice and talked to his shadow. It was a big shadow, a looming outline in the forest. He seemed truly surprised anyone was concerned as he followed us back to the truck. And he didn't seem to appreciate the effort that had been made on his behalf (or, as we saw it at the time, the effort made because of his foolishness).

Andy was partially right: Will had slipped into the woods with no gear or winter coat. And he had put an arrow into three pigs, and had gotten lost following the third one into the ice storm. Completely turned around, Will had managed to wade all the way through the deep water. When he reached high ground, he tripped over a pine lighter stump in the dark, then used his cigarette lighter to make a hot fire from the pitch-soaked wood. He broke down palmetto branches and built a shelter from the ice, snuggling in for the night until our horn honking and hollering woke him up. He was a woodsman, I'll give him that.

I was angry. Not at Will for getting lost, or even for him settling in all warm and cozy to sleep while we battled the sheriff, ice, Stoddard, and God. I was angry because he didn't seem to care about what we had been through. We made him sit in the bed of the truck in the wet ice while we drove. Our campmates had come out to search again as well, and we reached them on a cell phone with the good news.

In a few minutes Stoddard, Andy, and Danny were standing in the road ahead, backlit by headlights, waiting for us to drive out of the draw. They looked like executioners. Will stepped out of the truck bed toward them. Once Andy saw that Will was alive, he walked away from us all. He dropped to his knees on the wet ground in the glare of the lights and began to weep. He raised his arms and prayed in inconsolable sobs. His deep, throaty grief made Jimmy and me look at the ground and wish we could have just called the whole thing square and moved on. It was as if Will *had* died. After a bit, I walked to him and knelt down in the ice. I put an arm around him and breathed, "Andy, these should be tears of joy, not sorrow. Will's fine."

In a few minutes Andy picked himself up stiffly, with dignity. He got in his truck and drove back to camp, and never said a word to Will. Through the patter and slap of the icy rain I could hear Stoddard tell Will that he was forgiven. Then he took Will's arm as a father might and led him toward home, the highway, and his family. Camp became quiet. The weather broke with the dawn, and I could hear the ice turning to rain.

The next day I slept in long and hard. By the time I woke, the sun had asserted itself and cleared the skies with warm air. I was standing on the porch, coffee in hand, trying to drive the last chill out of my bones. A new hunter had arrived while I'd slept, and now he walked back into camp with my lost stone arrowhead in his hand. "Danny told me you lost an arrow and a little shoat pig in the swamp last night," he said, "so I went looking." He put a foot up on the porch and smiled. He held the arrow out to me. "Do you know how hard it was to find a little thing like this in that big swamp?"

I had a pretty good idea, but I just smiled back. "Nope," I said, "Tell me all about it."

Longbow

Drowning in the Sag

I had decided that my teenage son's strength and impulsive energy would complement my experience and seasoned judgment. In theory, John and I would be stronger as a team than as individuals. The whole is greater than the sum of its parts, isn't that the saying? An hour after I put that theory into practice it threw me off the back of a nine-foot rubber raft and held me underneath the freezing rapids of the Sag River, out of air and helpless. Welcome to the Arctic Circle.

My right foot was roped inside the raft's rigging and my body and head hung backwards over the stern. I was upside down and underwater. The raft spun clockwise in a whirlpool while I was drowning and freezing to death. In the flash of life that's supposed to pass before your eyes as you die, that final emptying of the brain vault that gives us time to repent or pray for mercy, I wasted my time wondering: *How did I get here?* The answer would have taken more time than I had left to give.

To Alaskans I'm an outsider. An interloper, a lower forty-eighter, a tourist. But I love it up there. Years ago I read Jay Massey's tales of rafting the Moose John River, about cold-edged campfires and the true compass that guides a hunter's heart. I wrote and asked him to help me tell my own stories. He wrote back and more. He called and advised and critiqued my words, and gave me his time for free. "Don't quit your day job," he laughed. Before long I was on my way to Anchorage to see the Moose John River for myself, through his eyes. In a few days Jay taught me to run a raft on the rapids, to pull wooden oars through cold brass locks on a rubber frame. I learned the basics: how to slip over logjams and break the fall ice. I was hooked. I was happy. I went home dreaming of the return engagement.

Not long after that trip Jay called late one night to tell me he was dying. We talked about Martha and Sophie, his wife and little girl, and I sat up over the edge of a dark brown glass the rest of the night. He died soon after. Months later Martha and Sophie came to see me. I gave Sophie pictures of her father and stories I had written about him, but I felt like I was opening a wound in that little girl's heart. She deserved better.

I never saw the Moose John again. I stayed away from Alaska. A few years later the Reverend Scotty Bennett invited me to Fairbanks, the northern edge of civilization. Scotty had been broken apart by drugs and drink and the lower forty-eight in his youth, but was reconstructed by the far north and God. He was eager to show them both to anyone needing salvation. Apparently he thought I fit the profile.

Scotty brought me north to chase caribou with longbows over the Brooks Range, above the Arctic Circle. Three landmarks travel the tundra like cousins from there to Prudhoe Bay: the Dalton Highway, the Alaska Pipeline, and the Sag river. When I saw the lonely Sag I knew I would return and float it north toward the Arctic Ocean. It turned gently through prime caribou grounds, close to the Dalton, but no one seemed to use it. I made plans the next year with my son John, just turned eighteen. We would return with Scotty to the Sag River above the Arctic Circle. Our float was to be a two-day test as part of a longer

Author and his son paying respects to the northernmost spruce in Alaska before their ill-fated first raft trip. Note the hatchet, which was not used.

land hunt on the tundra. In the meantime, I became a raft man.

Over the winter in Florida, I stacked up Redcrest rafts in my driveway like rednecks jack up Chevys: for use and parts. There may be better rafts for an Alaskan float trip, but I was emotionally attached to the Redcrest, the model that Jay used for the Moose John hunts. Rowing frames were another story. The Moose John frames were made of wooden staves, too large for commercial air travel. But I thought two men could build a frame from logs and wood found on the road, although there's a reason they call the tundra "treeless." Near the Brooks Mountain range, there's a sign that states: "Last spruce tree—do not cut."

North of that sign, the tundra has grass and bushes aplenty, but no trees or wood for frames, not unless it floats down the river or falls off a truck headed to Prudhoe Bay. My plan was to stock up on thin spruce logs where we could find them, and pick up a few wayward four-by-fours to lash together. I would make a natural frame for our maiden voyage. Today I build aircraft-aluminum frames that fit the requirements of commercial flight.

Of course, there were other essentials. My son John needed his bowhunter certificate (made easier since Scotty is an NBEF instructor). There were the logistics of bringing fuel, food, and camp supplies hundreds of miles north. And the Dalton Highway collapses in some spectacular manner nearly every year, stranding travelers behind sixty foot chasms of freezing water. Not to mention the weather, which in summer can visit every extreme of humidity and temperature over the course of a week. Snow and ice are guaranteed.

It all came together too easily. I should have been suspicious of otherworldly forces at work. I should have expected bad luck to balance out the good, and it did. Scotty, Dean Torges, John and I worked through three false starts as Scotty's Toyota trucks exploded on the Dalton one by one. The good Reverend finally rebuilt an engine overnight in his yard, under lights and a tarp and in a heavy snow. Come morning, Scotty swept a few leftover parts under the rug and off we went, only four days later than planned—not bad by Alaskan standards. Two days later we camped on the Sag near Prudhoe Bay, which is literally the end of the northern road.

With spruce saplings and castoff sign posts, my son and I pumped up a Redcrest and framed it to spread our weight over the tubes. We used paddles instead of oars. A frame of limbs and boards doesn't allow the luxury of rowing components. I thought we could do as well paddling the raft like a canoe. I was wrong.

I learned long ago that riding in a little boat is the surest path to ruining a relationship. Husband and wife or lifelong friends, it doesn't matter. The process of assigning tasks and blame while navigating a tippy little thing on the water always leads to "War of the Roses" types of confrontations. And I mean the dispute between England and France, not the divorce movie. With my son it was not much different. An overweighted raft sunk to its gunnels in freezing water is nearly impossible to paddle. Given that we were inexperienced southerners in unfamiliar waters, the risk was high. The result was predictable. In fact, it was foretold.

We finished the frame and pushed off on our two day forty-mile float, but our little Kon-Tiki took on water immediately. We saw opportunities to improve our condition, and dragged the raft ashore.

I don't know why—premonition, I suppose—but I stopped to go over "rules" with my son as we refitted and prepared to shove off. "If something bad happens," I said, "Do nothing. Stop and think first. If one of us falls out, the worst thing the other can do is to rush to help and tip the raft. That would kill us both." I drew on my old training as a firefighter. "Stop and take your own pulse. Let's talk through a plan before we do anything, okay?" My sense was that John was listening to that advice as well as he had listened to any other I had given him in his life (which is to say, not at all), but at least it had been said.

We pushed off again. Our gear and food was in dry bags, lashed to the saplings that made up the frame. There were lashing ropes aplenty, one of which nearly killed me. I was in the stern, John was in the bow. The raft handled much better, but I couldn't see the water ahead. We were not communicating well about rocks and rapids. John has always had a concern about water—short of a fear, as he will go swimming and into the ocean, but water makes him nervous. On the other hand I love rapids, and the bumps and swells on the Sag were fun to me. I headed for them while my boy tried to bypass. This further muddied the communication. We paddled in opposite directions most of the time.

Then the "thing" appeared. In the middle of the river, we both could see that something was in the water. It didn't look like a rapid or a rock. As with so many things in life, we talked about it until it was too late to do anything about it. When it became clear that we were floating toward a whirlpool, and a big one, we could no longer avoid it. We were headed straight for its center (a good technique to avoid rocks but not so effective on whirlpools). As life went into slow motion, the raft plowed over the edge into the sucking hole bow first and then right back up the other side. Our whole enterprise stood straight up on its stern at the apex of the climb, defying gravity. We were motionless for one breathless moment.

I was sitting on the stern underneath my son. It was clear that we were about to flip backwards, landing both of us upside down in the whirlpool. But I thought that if I pitched myself off the back, the sudden shift in weight might send the raft and John forward, out of danger. So over I went. The raft did in fact pitch forward with my son in it and slapped the river right side up. But on my way out my right foot was forced between two lines of lashing. My boot was trapped inside the raft.

I became a sea anchor, keeping us in the whirlpool. We spun around. I had the strength to raise my head above water (thank God for sit-ups), and see my obviously terrified son about to leap to my rescue.

"*Don't* move!" I gurgled, "Think it through. Don't tip the raft." He settled back down, tense and ready. "Geez, it's cold," I said over and over. My chest ached. It was thirty-six degrees, according to Scotty. I couldn't breathe, couldn't move, couldn't keep my head above water more than a moment. And I couldn't think past the cold.

"What do I do?" My son shouted, snapping me back to the problem at hand. But getting my thoughts into words was like pulling taffy.

"Get my foot free. Move slow!" I was losing strength fast.

"I can do that." I remember John saying, and I had no doubt that my weightlifter son would wrench my foot free.

I couldn't help him. He moved carefully to the stern, took hold of my boot, and turned my leg hard to the side. He popped my boot back through the rigging, and cast me free of the raft, which floated downstream from the whirlpool and me. My problem had become more personal. I couldn't stay afloat with my gear, my heavy wool coat, pack, gun and knives. The raft had been killing me, but it had also kept me afloat. I tried to swim, but I couldn't do it. I started to sink. Then I felt my son take hold of me with his strong outstretched hand and drag me back to the raft. I hung on the float, heaving. I grew up on the Canadian border. I spent my childhood wet and frozen in the wilds, but I had never been so cold or so completely spent.

John balanced the weight in the bow to avoid capsizing. I had to drag myself into the stern alone. It took many tries. After that I just lay there while he paddled us to shore. He started a fire and put up the tent, pulled off my clothes and jammed me inside the forty-below sleeping bag I had brought (overkill, some said, for the Alaskan summer). Our dry bags had done their job and protected all of our gear—I was the only thing wet and frozen. I warmed up without any residual effect, but the same couldn't be said for my son the next day.

"I'm not going back on that river," he said, clearly shaken. "What do you want me to do? Go home and tell mom I lost you in Alaska?" He stirred the fire, sending up sparks, fanning the flame.

"I want to go home."

Home was impossible. Anything but getting back on the river was impossible. We were prepared for a two-day float to our takeout point. We were not prepared for an overland expedition through the Alaskan wilderness. Unfortunately, John didn't want to hear about it.

It was hard to argue with him after he had just saved my life, but that's what it took. Hours of argument. When we did get back on the river, it was a slow, rapids-avoiding, conversation-free grind. Finding grizzly tracks in the snow over our footprints near the river didn't improve his mood. So I'm not sure which one of us was more excited about rounding a bend two days later to see Scotty and Dean waiting for us. I know I was joyful, glad to be alive. Our bows were still in watertight float tubes, where they had stayed the whole trip. I was soon able to work on my rusting sidearm and knife, both of which I still have and will always keep.

Jay and John Campbell just before shoving off on the Sag River, only to capsize in a whirlpool. Note the cobbled-together raft seats and braces. Rigging from the logs caught the author's leg and nearly killed him.

In hindsight, I've lost count of the boneheaded decisions I made. I let the joy of the adventure overwhelm my sense of systems and safety. I exposed my son to those dangers, not just myself. We were lucky. Today, and just as a start to the list of required items, I would provision us with personal flotation devices, satellite communication gear, and precision rowing frames. It was a hard decision to return.

But I went back the next year and the year after. I love it there. As for John, I'm still working on him. The experience brought us together, but not so close that he will return to the river. By the time he's forty or so, I hope to get him back on the river for one last float with his father. Or maybe when he's fifty, and I'm eighty.

Then, he just might figure that drowning me in the Sag would be doing me a favor.

Longbow

A Goat Too Far

On the crest of the Island of Isla Mona, between Puerto Rico and Costa Rica, a Spanish goat took my cane arrow to the edge of a Caribbean cliff. He was supper, and I was interested in him as meat, not a trophy. The butchering went fast, leaving a cape and carcass behind a devil-horned head. It occurred to me then that there was still a use for the remains.

Mona Island bursts out of the Atlantic Ocean tall and clean, as straight on her sides as a can of soup. On the island's highest edge, I straddled the goat and looked down a dizzying drop to the sea. It seemed an immense height. I wanted to know exactly how high I had climbed to chase my dinner, and I decided to use the goat—or rather its remains—as an altimeter.

I braced against a small tree and threw the scruffy corpse off the island ledge. I used my watch to count the seconds, marking time until impact with the ocean. It seems perverse now no matter how I relate it, but at the time it was an act of island alchemy I was quite proud of.

I counted six-and-one-half seconds before the goat met the Atlantic. If my math was right ($Height = \frac{1}{2} Gravity \times Time^2$), I was standing 210 feet above the ocean. I rested a few moments before climbing down the cliffs with my meat, the image of exploding goat vivid in my mind.

I was a veteran of Isla Mona, having survived three island tours. Years before my first, in bars near the docks of San Juan, tales of Isla Mona were shared like rum in church—quietly, under the table, as if someone was watching. It was the lair of *El Chupacabra, the Goat-Sucker,* seamen said, and a smuggler's cove for "go-fast" boats guarded by trigger-happy opportunists. Latino newspapers were full of it. On Mona Island, hard men covered bad deals with fast guns.

In libraries and law firms, places I loitered back then until the bars opened, educated men knew Isla Mona as the intersection of world history. Christopher Columbus, Ponce De Leon, Captain Kidd, and the architect Eiffel had all seen the beaches, caves and cliffs of Mona Island. But the modern Mona Island was abandoned. The modern Isla Mona was also overrun with wild goats and pigs, descendants of Spanish animals put ashore for a renewable food supply. This made her the only choice for hunting the Caribbean with my longbow.

Hunting Mona was easier said than done. The Department of Natural Resources in Puerto Rico doesn't allow applications by mail or online. On every trip my friends and I were required to go in person with no guarantee of being awarded the permits. We flew into San Juan, waded through the permit process, drove across the island to Boqueron, and chartered a stout boat for the fifty mile crossing to Isla Mona. Once there, our boat the *Orca Too* would leave and return after the hunt to take us home. It is a difficult, cumbersome journey now. Centuries ago it must have been torture.

I landed on Isla Mona five hundred years after Columbus cast off. It's much the same today as then, insulated from the world by drought and blue water. Columbus found a ragged group of Taino natives when he arrived, who did not survive the Europeans for long. Captain Kidd hid in Mona's blue lagoons, lounging under coconut palms. He should have stayed on the beach. Kidd was taken to England and hanged not once, but three times. The rope broke on the first two drops. Gustave Eiffel designed the nameless Mona lighthouse as well as his namesake Paris tower and New York's Statue of Liberty. The lighthouse stands rusted now, listing and ready to fall, the beacon glass shattered and strewn in piles. Spanish and American miners excavated bat guano from the deep caves in the 1800s, chiseling out excrement two meters deep, driving the bats away forever. Railroad iron still crosses the island heights, from caves to cliffs above hulking iron boilers on the beaches. Nitrates were boiled out of bat dung and ferried away for fertilizer. Since then, except for hunters in December, only an overmatched group of armed rangers live on the island.

Isla Mona is part of the Commonwealth of Puerto Rico, the United States' most eastern shore. It is a smuggler's waypoint from all points south. Firefights and bloody bundles of cocaine are the island's modern legends, which make hunting there interesting, at the least. The island is also known as the "Galapagos of the Caribbean" for its stunning wildlife.

Mona's history, exciting as it is, is no match for her beaches. Whenever I stepped ashore, the strain of the planning and the travel drained into the wet white sand between my toes. Broad-leaf palms bent down for shade, and I always quickly fell asleep beneath one. Each time I had earned the rest, banging from wave to wave before dawn until our chain-smoking captain Paco slipped the *Orca* through a narrow cut to shore.

This time I had dropped my gear on the beach, waved goodbye to Paco and climbed the crumbling lighthouse for the view. I glassed my old landmarks but little had changed. The west side of the island was not where I wanted to be. Mona is seven miles across, with most of the middle too thick for travel. But there is one path from the west beach to the east beach, and I wanted to be on it before dawn. Paco had given me a lead on goats on the east side of the island.

I began the hike at midnight on a moonless night. It was four hours of hard walking until I was wrapped in the sound of waves again. From Mona's eastern beach I still had a stiff two-hour climb to the northern cliffs in the dark. Paco said goats schooled there like tropical fish, sweeping from cactus to cactus. But Paco believed in *Chupacabras*, too. I hoped he could be as right about one thing as he was wrong about another.

Mona's rocks give a hollow, metallic ping when struck by boot or stone. Paco promised I would find goats by the music of their hooves,

Author and his "Altimeter" goat on Isla Mona's tallest cliffs.
Behind is Isla Monita, Isla Mona's little sister island. Camp was a bruising seven mile hike away.

the herds ringing as if they were collared and belled. I hoped to be in a concert of goats when shooting light came, but when I finished my climb I was alone in the dark and tired. I didn't believe him anymore.

On the highest point of the island, I slumped behind a collapse of stone and waited. Cactus spines pierced my boots and hands, making for a prickly bed. I stood and tweezed out my new piercings while I waited for the waves of goats Paco had promised me. I fingered the Osage wood bow in my hand, an unbacked longbow with a handle wrapped in stingray hide, a fitting weapon for where I sat. My arrows were feathered cane gathered from Florida swamps, likely similar to those used by the original Taino natives on Mona. I had a brace of self-knapped stone heads in my quiver, backed up with all-steel, two-blade broadheads on the rest of the cane arrows. I had practiced with this gear in the heat and wet of Florida for years. I was confident in my tropical choices. I liked the feel of the wood and leather in my hands in such a desolate place.

At first light hollow rings played in the air above the high stone fields, just as Paco said. The melody moved toward me. Sea birds circled as I waited. The sun sharpened their wings as they flared to land.

Split hooves rang closer on the hollow rocks as I hid. Three dozen Spanish goats appeared in the rock field below me. Billies, nannies, and kids swarmed the wet cactus, tearing green pulpy pads free, beards dripping. The Atlantic was backstage as the brown herd fed between me and the ocean, brilliantly blue in the early light. I chose the closest rather than the largest, as is my habit. I released a flint arrow at twenty steps, my Osage bow bending back and flexing forward without a sound.

A sound came after the shot, but it was more of a crack than the thump I expected. The nanny and I stared at each other, neither of our mornings shaping up according to plan. My arrow lay between us, still pointing at the goat, having bounced off her and landed on the rocks. She trotted off without a limp. I picked up my stone arrow and felt the flint tip that had been broken by the goat's shoulder. This ended my experiment in Caribbean stone head hunting. I pulled a new arrow with a steel head from my quiver and took up the trail.

The goat was wary, but not frightened. Few Mona animals have ever seen people. They have no predators above the waterline. My nanny was still close, grazing, chewing, dripping into her beard. Cactus gave me grudging cover while I watched for cave openings on the surface. I had seen one already, manhole sized, twenty feet deep. When the nanny stopped to feed I sent a new cane arrow through both lungs, collapsing her in place. The herd rang away to their caves, taking their stone music with them.

I was alone then, the new corpse my only company. The birds had swooped off and gone silent, the musical hooves had hushed. The crash of the sea below worked its way into my head, competing with my heavy breathing.

A feeling came over me then that always does when I take an animal. I used to feel it only as a lonely let-down after the chase and the adrenaline rush. But that day I felt it differently. I felt it as a sense of belonging, a calm understanding that my position in the world had been affirmed. In the farthest reaches I had ever hunted, so distant from my own land and my own people, I knew my place. I was a hunter.

I shouldered twenty pounds of purple island meat and stood sweating in the Caribbean sun. I had a long hot return over Isla Mona's middle ahead of me, but I wasn't alone. Columbus was keeping me company.

Easy Does It

In March our New Mexico home was choked in the brown dust of the high desert winter. The wind scoured our treeless mountain plains, whipping dirt and snow from one arroyo to the next. Don Davis had given Karen and me a wedding present of a longbow pig hunt, so we took our spring where we could find it. We flew east to Florida, where the Sunshine State was everything New Mexico was not: lush, green, and wet. The tropic woods were blooming.

Don's camp was buckled into a grove of oaks in the plumb-bob center of the state. Spanish moss swept the wood-planked porch of his cabin. Wild oranges bent close enough to reach, and I ate sweet slices until my lips buzzed. Under a broad beam of sun with orange juice on my chin, I melted into my chair and slept through the afternoon. For a few hours, hunting became an afterthought.

We were on the Woodson lease, the richest reserve in the state, and Don was allowing us to wander and make our own mistakes. The next morning, long before dawn, Karen pulled on big rubber boots and oversized clothes from the old mismatched camo I had brought along. It was her first hunt of any kind. It was also the first time she had taken her longbow off the target range.

We waded from camp through a cypress head into pastures rooted apart by pigs. We sat in the high grass in the dark. When the sun came up, shoats squealed over food in the distance, tussling closer. I happily sounded out: "Pigs are close," and heard a whispered, unhappy, "Oh no!" in return. When I turned around my expression must have asked for an explanation. My new wife leaned in close to me and, with a small voice, barely a whisper, she confided, "I'm *scared* of pigs."

Now? I thought. You're telling me *now?*

Whether she was scared or not, the pigs were feeding toward us. As Karen saw it, we had no choice but to run away. Her fear caused us to conduct a hurried exchange on our knees in the grass about pig attack survival rates; the average land speed of hogs; whether she or I was faster in the sprint; and, my hope that she would, if she survived, communicate such important concerns sooner in the future. It was a spirited talk, but it did not slow the impending encounter between pigs and persons.

Piggy shadows gradually appeared through the grasses and fog. Karen watched them feed and chase about as pigs do. They slowly moved closer. She got used to the pigs and her fears. There were five mature boars together, a little Band of Brothers walking into our unraveling ambush. The group stopped at twenty yards. Karen gathered her courage and stood up to shoot. As she later said: "I was so shocked by not one, but two pigs standing completely still less than twenty yards away, giving me a clear shot while I was standing up, that I promptly shot my arrow into the ground right in front of me." That about covered it. Off the pigs ran while I laughed, she got mad, and she gathered up her arrow and chased after them, scared no more. When she returned we walked back to camp and shared our mistakes over a good dinner and red wine.

Don's friends quickly become our friends. Woody Woodson, Chip Turknett, and Craig Courty generously shared their supper. There are many kitchens in that grand old camp, and there need to be. Breakfast and dinner on the Woodson Lease are stage productions. Craig Courty is the producer and master chef, coordinating every course. One kitchen can't keep enough food flowing for the twenty members and guests who usually eat together. Appetizers, entrees, and desserts are farmed out to willing members who deliver serving dishes timed to the minute in Craig's dinner choreography. Duck breasts stuffed with hot peppers were marinating over there in Chip's oven. Tenderloins of bacon-wrapped venison were broiling over here on Craig's grill. Woody's thick cream blueberry pies waited in his outdoor cooler, firm and cold for dessert, while Don Davis mixed fresh sour-orange margaritas before the dinner bell. We were overwhelmed by the attention, stuffed beyond moving, and we slept soundly through the morning hunt as a result.

We scouted the next day until sunset, when we glassed swampy fields until pigs filled the lenses—all sizes and colors of pigs, two hundred yards away. Karen asked me to take the long stalk over open pasture to show how it was done. I crawled most of the way through cow pies and grass clumps until my fingers began to sizzle and burn. My hands had slipped into a nest of fire ants. But with Karen and the pigs watching me, I held still. I wasn't going to impress my new wife or a pig by squealing and slapping at my hands like a schoolgirl. Even though I wanted to.

The pigs were calm, pulling up roots under the hazy orange sunset. I lifted my hands and rasped the vibrating little biters off on saw grass. *Calm down*, I reminded myself, *Take your own pulse*. I rested a bit, then finished crawling within thirty steps of a sow, longbow in my swollen left hand, two feathered arrows in my stiffening right. I like to be closer. But pigs were ranging all around me, and their radar was too

Karen Campbell rabbit hunting in the New Mexico Desert, soon after she married the author.

thick. I had practiced the shot for years - on my knees, bent down behind cover, bow horizontal to the ground. It's hard to reach full draw and hit the anchor properly in that position with a seventy-five-pound bow, but I picked a spot behind the pig's shoulder and released the arrow cleanly.

The shaft slipped through the dry sow broadside. She dropped in place. I moved up quickly, scattering the nursing sows and football-sized shoats that were milling around in confusion. Karen ran up behind me, out of breath, speaking in bursts: "That was so exciting," she exhaled. "Look at all these pigs!" Then she paused, giving me an expectant look. "Can *I* shoot one?" I nodded and off she went, chasing pigs in the tall brush, leaving me shaking my head. I sat alone with my pig in the fading light, looking forward to a future with my bowhunting wife where life, and hunting, was going to be easy.

Longbow

Karen's Heart

We flew back to the Florida coast in April, where the air was still cool and oranges overfilled the roadside stands. We drove east on Highway 60 from Tampa. Karen kept the windows down, feeling the breeze as the scenery shifted from beach sand to ranch land. In Tampa bellhops laughed at our rough hunting duffels, but camouflage is welcome in the center of the Sunshine State.

Yeehaw Junction sits where State roads 60 and 441 meet, and marks Florida's middle with a single blinking light. The name seems to holler *Dixie*, and conjures up visions of loose livestock and Confederate flags. A few banty roosters run wild, but the folks nearby are friendly, with simple values rooted in the land. In Central Florida if you *hunt* you're family, whether you live above or below the Mason-Dixon Line. Karen and I stopped calling our longbow cases "fishing rods," pulled on camo clothes in the Quik-Stop restroom, and got nods of approval from everyone we met.

Just north of the Junction, our camp was a cluster of shacks and buggies in a thick oak swamp. It was lush and tangled and loud. The critters hammered, chattered and gobbled nonstop, but it all became a pleasant hum after a while, like the white noise of traffic. Further from camp the woods quieted into a bowhunter's dream for Karen.

Athena sprang from Zeus' brow with her bow in hand, ready to hunt. It takes mortal women a bit longer to master the bow. My wife had picked up a longbow for the first time only a year earlier. She was fluent in the fundamentals, but she had missed her first chance at a pig a month before. On this trip, she was determined to connect.

My first animal didn't fall for years after I picked up a bow, so I had prepared Karen for disappointment on our last trip. Even so, I thought her first miss might make her quit the hunt. I was wrong. The failure drove her harder until she was the one energizing me with her excitement. That is, once I could get her out of bed. Even on the first morning of this second trip, Karen acted as if I had never disclosed that waking up early was part of the hunting experience. Chip Turknett's thick camp coffee put her mostly upright and us mostly out the door just before sunrise, walking in the mist near a strand of black water. Once again, we were chasing Florida wild pigs.

Wild pigs are a destructive foreign force in North America, like kudzu. They are unstoppable omnivores. Smart, social, and adaptable, hogs range free almost everywhere, but Florida is their homeland. The first Spanish explorers loosed pigs from wooden ships in the 1500s. European genes mold the muscular shoulders, small hips, and ivory tusks that distinguish wild pigs from their barnyard cousins. They are wary, tough animals to hunt, wonderful on the table, and they owned the Florida jungle around our camp.

Fences, scrub brush and oaks appeared here and disappeared there in the rolling gray distance. Coyotes howled. We stood cold in the dark. We shook our stiff bones loose, waiting for the light to reveal a stick or clod of dirt worth the effort of a practice arrow. We waited for the wind to turn but at dawn the breeze was still on our backs, giving us no chance to surprise pigs. We walked along regardless. A mile later the travel and the short night and the walk began to wear us down, and a nap became important—more important than the morning hunt. But sometimes, pigs happen.

When the first pig squealed, we glanced at each other with real disappointment. This was a temporary insanity I blame on some form of piggy stress disorder… *Dysphoria Porcinus*. Even sleep-deprived pig hunters should feel good about finding pigs. But if hearing pigs caused the syndrome, seeing them cured it. When two sows and a dozen large shoats shuttled out of the swamp in front of us and ripped into a patch of purple-flowered clover, we sprang into action. We couldn't have avoided them if we wanted to.

Karen asked to go it alone. I watched her make a plan, mentally assessing everything she had seen me do the month before. She quietly implemented her checklist: fanny pack off—*check*; quiver on the ground—*check*; spare arrow in her string hand—*check*. She asked my advice about cover, but there were seventy yards of flat pasture between us and them. Her only protection was their poor vision. "Crawl?" I shrugged, and off she went on hands and knees. I wasn't much help.

I raised four children, so I know about separation anxiety. Not theirs but mine. I remember the knot of pride and loss I felt when my children walked alone to school, rode away on a two-wheel bike, or left my arm at their weddings. I thought I was past that feeling at my age, but when Karen crawled away it all came back to me. *My new wife, hunting pigs all on her own.* I set up my camera and settled back to watch, feeling quite useless.

The feeling didn't last long. I clipped a big lens onto my camera. I expected I would have time to take pictures of a long, slow stalk. It didn't happen. I snapped one shot and picked up my tripod to get closer when Karen drew her bow, held for a very long time, and released an arrow in the general direction of the pigs.

I heard a thump, and the plan quickly unraveled. Pigs scattered past me back to the swamp. Karen shouted "I hit it!" and vaulted a barbed wire fence to chase them down. I tried not to drop a mortgage payment's worth of camera lens into a cow pie. I realized then that we had never really discussed what to do if she shot an animal, since I didn't really think she would hit one. When Karen watched me take a pig, the animal had dropped in place—a one in a hundred result—so there were no lessons about post-hit protocols or blood trailing. When she hit her pig all I could think to do was yell "Stop!" and make the universal sign for . . . well . . . *stop*. Thrusting out my hands, I felt like a traffic cop. She stopped, but there was obviously a different hand gesture she wanted to return.

In a few seconds I met Karen where her arrow met the pig. I was full of questions and she was full of answers, but the two weren't related in any meaningful way. I suppose we were speaking different languages. Hers was the tongue of her first hunting strike, an emotional, lyrical dialect. Mine was analytical, more suited to dissecting the hit and planning the blood trail. We were on different communication planets - *Mars and Venus*.

Using hand signals and other signs, the basic story came out: At twenty yards Karen had loosed a good arrow and hit a ninety-pound pig broadside in the center of the chest. *Good.* As I mentally began to translate my questions about her arrow, I looked down and found it buried in the ground at my feet, feathers blood soaked, a pass-through shot. *Better.* Karen said the pigs had bolted into the swamp fifty yards away under a fence line. *Bad.* No matter how good the hit, I never want to trail an animal through swamp.

We were still in the pasture studying her arrow when a long, single squeal pealed from the strand. A death moan. Hearing it, Karen's

Karen Campbell with her first Florida pig, on the 10,000 acre Woodson lease she and the author shared with 12 other hunters.

face began to reflect the hunt from the pig's point of view—a feeling many hunters share when taking their first animal. "Is he dead?" she asked quietly. A nod was answer enough, and we returned to the forensics of finding the body.

I walked her to the wire fence where the high grass would swipe blood from a wounded animal ducking under. We each took a side and quietly walked along the line in tandem. We found crossing red smears within a few minutes. Then Karen took over the trail—her last test. This was an open-book exam. The animal was seeping from both sides, leaving splotches left and right. She bent down and tracked slowly for thirty yards, asking questions while I held back to let her stutter-start off the track now and then, always picking it up again alone. The trail grew bolder and she moved faster and farther ahead of me. Then she suddenly stepped back with her hands to her chest, exhaling a sad, soft, "Oh my God."

At that moment I wondered where her heart would turn. My wife had never taken an animal before. Most hunters feel empathy for the game they hunt, but not everyone can take a life and keep their emotions in perspective. Her eyes lowered to the ground for a moment as we stood there, then she raised them to the animal intently and asked, "Where did I hit him?" I smiled to myself and I knew then where she would turn.

Karen had a hunter's heart.

When Fish Fly

In the Wisconsin summer I was basking in the morning sun by my little lake, the Waubeesee, near the town of Muskego. Karen and I opened the morning mail, making plans and small talk. Life was good. We sorted through the bills and fliers until a test result slipped from a laboratory envelope, unexpected, uninvited, and unwelcome. Time stopped.

I have never understood why the human body, usually so good at self-defense, switches our senses to slow motion for life's worst moments, yet speeds them beyond remembrance for the best of them. It is a failure of evolution I would like to discuss with Darwin.

That was my life's worst moment. My new wife and I were frozen at the kitchen table by one word on that single piece of paper - *cancer*. I was unable to move while the word bore down hard. It plowed into me like a runaway train. It launched me into motion. In thirty days Karen and I saw twelve doctors in four states. They were all of one mind: the tumor was growing fast, I needed surgery soon, and surgery might not be enough.

*Jay Campbell bowfishing in Wisconsin just before cancer surgery.
Photo by Karen Campbell.*

I couldn't buy a different opinion. I tried. I had MRIs, CAT scans, biopsies and nuclear dyes, and was left radioactive enough for nuclear fission. Every test confirmed the diagnosis. We chose a hard course of action that stiffened at each turn: surgery, readmission, more surgery, drugs. As the nightmare unfolded we decided to enjoy ourselves if life would allow it. For us, that meant hunting, and adventure, and longbows.

I've been drawing back longbows since I first stretched a string between the ends of a yardstick, flinging pencils into a target on my mother's couch. Richard Greene was *Robin Hood* on our black and white TV, my boyhood hero. Errol Flynn's *The Adventures of Robin Hood* and Howard Hill's classic book *Hunting the Hard Way* were my most beloved childhood entertainment. I pored over the Bear archery catalog in the bathroom the way most kids ogled the lingerie section of the Sears Book. Hunting with the longbow had been my lifelong joy, and joy is strong medicine for the things that ail you. Karen and I sorted our priorities, and made room for the healing power of the sport.

I engaged my bucket list early. I hoped to do it all before things became worse. Thirty days before surgery Karen and I began to hunt like there might not be a thirty-first. Friends helped us do it. Places became plans, someday became today, and I revised my date book more often than an Iraqi invasion plan. Friends also helped us plan for a life after surgery.

Before the cancer Karen and I had hunted in Florida with E. Donnall Thomas, a physician and always a friendly voice of reason. We talked about buffalo in Australia for the next summer, but he had vetoed Karen hunting with us—she was too new to hunting, he argued, her fifty-pound longbow too weak. I understood, but I chose to stay home with my new wife. After the cancer Don wrote a hunting prescription, and I will always be grateful:

"Cripes, Jay, you drew a bad hand," he griped on my behalf. *"But I'm going to help you through it. It's all about the future. I've changed my mind about Karen hunting buffalo next summer. You get well and you get her ready, and I'll guide her myself. Fair enough?"*

It was more than fair. Karen cautiously climbed aboard Don's proposition, although she had not been consulted. She was a bit... well ... *concerned* about buffalo. And she had a harder job than I did. She had to draw a buffalo bow within a year. I only had to survive cancer.

Don's prescription was well-made. After my first operation, I mulled over that buffalo hunt every day. I lay awake in the hospital when I could barely breathe, calculating the force-draw curves of heavy bows and weighty arrows, making mental travel arrangements, gear lists, taxidermy consults, and the like. More than any single thing except my wife, the anticipation of that hunt lifted me over the hurdles of recovery. It gave Karen and me something to talk about when my prospects dimmed, new surgeries were required, and words were hard to find.

Don must have often rethought his offer, but Karen worked hard to meet his expectations. Six months after my last operation, my black-belt wife could pull a seventy-pound longbow gracefully. She was more prepared to meet a buffalo than I was.

But back in early June, the days before surgery had begun to squeeze together. Karen and I found new hunts, new reasons to stay afield and think of pleasant things. We chased Barbary sheep in New Mexico, scrambling those rimrock cliffs nearly fast enough to catch one. My stamina made the looming surgery harder to accept. It was one of the most difficult things about my diagnosis. I was never sick, never had symptoms. The tumor was found by chance, unexpected, like a cockroach in a cupcake. After the operations I would finally feel as sick as my doctors said I was, but it was cold comfort.

When Fish Fly

Dr. Thomas' archery recovery program spread east. Don Davis had hosted us on his ten-thousand acre Florida lease, gridlocked with wild oranges, turkey, and deer. He was perversely proud of the usual ten-year wait for membership. But when Don learned I was sick, my good friend proposed the *Widow* Campbell for a membership vote. "It's only a little ahead of schedule," he winked to the boys. My prospective widow was adopted by the lease members in a sympathy landslide, and we began to hunt on our new lease as soon as I could walk. Today those Florida hunts are the best therapy I have, and keep me focused on recovery. Our lease mates may expect my wife alone at the camp table soon, but every day I hunt is another day that I'm healthy. I expect to keep them waiting.

In late June my surgery was as inevitable as taxes, but we stole time for a final outing. The day of my last biopsy we drove to Illinois from Wisconsin to bowfish the Ohio River. We climbed onto an airboat under a full moon, up to our noses in exhaust. Racks of spotlights probed the river, but nothing moved in the dark water. Nothing at all. Still, Captain Chris Cass shouted over the engines: "Swells of big carp will break out of the wake beside us," he hollered. "They'll be fast targets moving through the surface into the air—flying fish in Illinois! Hit them just before they leap." We didn't really believe him, but we nocked our arrows, standing on bowed and unsteady legs. The air freshened out on the open water. It was loud and warm, but pleasant to be floating away from trouble. I felt like Huck, floating down the river to Cairo, to freedom.

The boat reached along the shore, negotiating shoals and shallows. Not a fin rippled. I relaxed a bit, disbelieving, watching bugs in the lights. Like my little league son I was focused on insects in the field, not the count against the batter. But I was having fun, no matter the distraction. It was good to be alive anywhere, even if fish couldn't really fly.

On the fourth pass the boat's bottom popped, just once. Then a follow-up second and third "pop" became a rattling on the hull, like hail on a tin roof. A school of silver carp was going airborne, but the first ones rammed the boat's hull in a flying frenzy. Captain Chris sent us to ready stations with a yahoo: "Here they come!" He let the wheel spin free while he took up his own bow, and fish blew into the air. Cat-sized carp flew over the boat and past us, some landing in the boat in a bloody splash. Spray ran from their tails to the surface, the drops frozen under the lights until they hit the deck and exploded. We traded fish-eyed stares face-to-face, more surprised than the carp to be sharing the atmosphere.

Karen and I were as out of our element as the fish were out of theirs. We hadn't had the sense to send an arrow into that first wave. When we stopped laughing and regrouped, the boat pressured schools against the shore again. More fish flew. I released and retrieved my fiberglass arrow a dozen times before I speared a silver carp on the rise, which dove and ran out the line. Fixed with a harpoon, he still played me more than I played him. It was a team struggle to bring him back. Karen hauled my line hand over hand while I reeled it in, the two of us navigating the carp around propellers, weeds, and rocks until she gaffed it and heaved it aboard. We took more fish with the boat than with arrows. In each attack two or three landed on the deck, slapping themselves silly against the hull until it was slippery red with roe and blood. We gaffed those gift fish into barrels just as if we had caught them honestly. Two drums were full when the sky lightened.

In the morning we jabbered about the trip like school kids on a bus. My wife was blood-stained, egg-smeared, and happy about it—not a predictable result in our neatly-ordered household. Anyone who would listen heard our fish story retold until they begged off. The excitement carried us to the admissions desk in a San Diego hospital a few days later. Then the doors to the surgical ward closed behind me, and my life took a hard turn south.

That all-night fishing trip the day of my last biopsy didn't make my surgeon happy. Doctor Carol Salem put a sharp edge on dull words like "moderation" and "common sense" and dissected my choices to the bone. But I would do it again. I have never had a time like the day we spent dodging flying carp. Days like that keep my thoughts in the moment, where life is still good. With enough days like that ahead of me, it may stay that way.

If fish can fly, anything can happen.

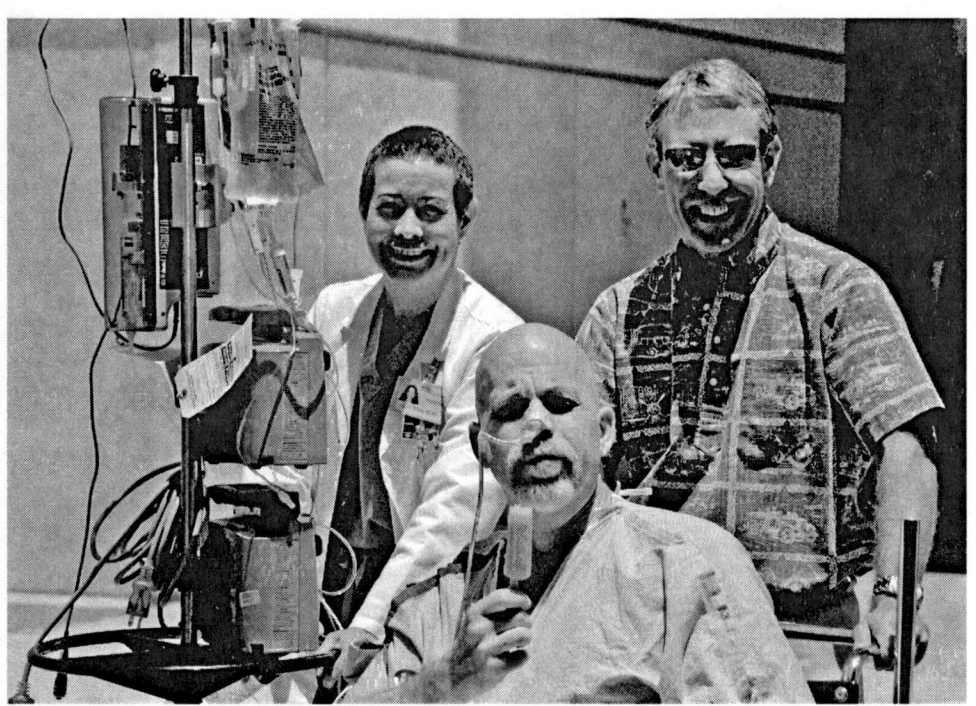

Author on the first day he was allowed outside after cancer surgery, accompanied by cardiologist Dr. Laura Pinderski, hospital CEO Bryan Rogers, and a cherry popsicle. The hospital stay was two weeks and multiple trips to the O.R., all while thinking about Dr. Thomas' promised buffalo hunt. Photo by Karen Campbell.

Longbow

Virgil's Lion

The arroyo behind my home drains the Sandia Mountain foothills through the high desert. It's whipped by dust and tumbleweeds in the dry season, although it always seems to be the dry season in New Mexico.

On the mountain's softer side, other homes are favored with gentle slopes and rain, pine forests and streams. But we live on the dry side of the mountain, under dusty cliffs that shred the air like pot shards. No extreme bike or board could run our mountain slope, which is just as well. Life stays quiet. Mule deer bed in our front yard, unruffled by the coyotes and bobcats that cross our drive in the sidelight of morning. They are all protected by the same covenants that keep the desert wild around our home, and it's a fair trade.

We live in this pocket of New Mexico under the shadow of the Sandia, on the edge of a wilderness area. But true wilderness is history here. Black bears are so rare they make bylines, and mountain lions are memories, soon to be forgotten like the grizzlies that owned this desert 150 years ago. A few hundred yards away we spill out onto the Albuquerque Tramway, which funnels me quickly to the international airport. Our once-wild place has become civilized, but not too far away the mountain desert is still as hardscrabble and hard to tame as it was a century ago, when it was settled by men and women as rough as the stone they lived on. Many of them still live there.

Butch Wilks has been hunting and trapping the mountains of New Mexico for almost all of his fifty-some years. He trapped the desert around our home before there were houses, when he took lions and mule deer. When the contractors moved in, Butch moved out, looking for a wild place to hunt and trap the high desert. He found it a hundred miles to the east, where New Mexico ranchers still own parcels defined by thousands of square miles, on land so rough and dry it can't support corporate buyers. Sons of grandsons of homesteaders live where their families settled one hundred and fifty years ago, where oral histories

Jay Campbell and Mountain Man Butch Wilks in the lion's den while sheep hunting near Corona, New Mexico. Note the deer skeletons. Photo by Karen Campbell.

of drought, Indian wars, and large predators are still real and personal. Butch took Karen and me to meet Virgil Owen. We were going to hunt Barbary sheep and small game on his land, on a place where big cats still own the mountains.

Virgil Owen walks like a man out of step with doctor's orders. A veteran of war and world travel, he's tolerant enough of friends and family, but strangers get a raised brow over a sharp eye. He's as spare and dry as the land he owns. Under the rimrock cliffs near Cougar Mountain, the Owen family settled hard land that spreads farther than a man can see in any direction. Little has changed since then, despite engines and electricity. He was born on the second of three homesteads on the ranch, and lives in the third with his wife, Shirley. The children are gone to bigger cities, modern life. On an early weekday morning, Virgil allowed us in for beer and "sweetener," a cold can of Coors topped with warm Canadian Club. Since Butch had spoken up for Karen and me, Virgil was willing to talk about water, life, and lions.

On Virgil's earth the value of a thing is measured in moisture. He knows the evaporation rates of holding tanks and the output of his windmills like they were his children's birthdays. The rain stopped falling two generations ago. Wet fields that flowered beans and melons in his childhood sprout dust devils now. Under the eaves of his grandmother's stone hut, the deep water turned acid. Cows will die of thirst before they drink it. The family has chased fresher water in deeper wells across the ranch twice since then, ending up in their new home, the center of operations. They have fewer cows, less feed, and more work, but Virgil makes it go with an engineer's eye and faith.

Hunting has become part of ranching now. Virgil sold his hunting rights to a Texas consortium, reserving only the right for Butch to chase deer and Barbary sheep now and then. But lions have begun to eat into the thin margins of his ranching business.

"In three years we've lost more stock to lions than in the last twenty." He gestured through a truck window, moving us from his kitchen to the mesa. "There's game and cows lying out there now that this one old cat leaves dead where they lay." He smiled. "Go ahead and kill him if you get a chance."

We left Virgil and wandered into the rimrock. From the high cliffs deep in Virgil's ranch, we glassed deer, cows, and Barbary sheep lying below us in a narrow gorge. "He's killing because he likes it," Butch said. We had come to chase Barbary sheep with longbows, but the only sheep we saw were lion kills. They were on display in the open like he was marking his territory.

A day introduced by fifty years of drought should be as dry as bones, but New Mexico weather has a contrary nature. Black clouds furled quickly out of the west, and fingered the cliffs with electricity. Heat and color drained from the air like a vein had been opened. When the hair on our necks stood up, we ran off the high ledges. Balls of rain blew dust spouts at our feet and lightning slapped the high ground. We scrambled to safety. The storm raced by, passing over Virgil's land to water some other man's farm, someone else's more fortunate cows.

Down in the gorge we took stock of the dead. The kills were clean, uneaten. They lay every few hundred yards. "No coyote would leave carcasses like this," Butch said. He glassed up the slope to find a high-walled cave with a ribcage for a welcome mat. The lion's den. "Jay, if you and Miss Karen want to, we can climb up above that den and come down on top of him for a look-see." Butch made the offer as if he were asking us to dinner.

Karen agreed to go, but she refused to lead into the cave. That would be my job, apparently. We climbed high again. At the top, Karen was ahead when her left hand tightened on the grip of her longbow. Her right eased a broadhead free, and she waved us down into a crouch. I was thinking lions.

The desert in New Mexico is a thing of beauty, if you take time to stretch and relax, like this Ground Squirrel in the Sandia Mountains.

"Bunnies," she whispered.

When we appeared on top of the mesa, jackrabbits came unhinged. They bounded like pinballs through pods of cactus, going all at once in every direction and nowhere at all. They seemed more kangaroo than rabbit, sailing by us on the up or downswing of their furry arcs, slapping the sand with both feet and flying away again. It was not clear how to hunt them without hurting ourselves. One finally stood frozen, ears twitching a yard high. It made a tough, distant shot. At thirty yards, Karen locked her eyes on that tall target and knocked him ass over teawhistle with her first arrow. Humbled, I fetched her prize and turned my attention back to the more manly pursuit of lions.

I made no sneak on the lion's cave. I was graveyard cautious, kicking rocks ahead of me down the slope. The mouth of the cave opened just below the steep lip of the mesa. I swallowed hard at the smell. It was a bad mix of cat box and slaughterhouse gases. Goat, sheep, and deer parts were crosshatched one over another in the shadows, in all stages of rot. This cat would lay on piles of bones, guarding his old kills and choosing new ones from above. He was a calculating killer. We stayed a moment to take pictures but hiked away smartly in the shadows, watching our back trail.

In the softening light we rested on a high rock ledge, watching Virgil work below us. During the day we had seen him at a distance here and there, repairing pumps, mending fence, always in motion. Now he was throwing white fertilizer by hand, ferrying fifty pound bags from the tractor. His hands and face were caked, making him look paler still. Virgil works hard to make his family ranch prosper. The rogue cat was killing stock. It cost Virgil money. I wondered why it was still running free. I asked Butch why Virgil hadn't killed the lion, but he didn't answer. I let it go. Maybe, I thought, he didn't know where the big cat lived. Later we could map the den for him, and Virgil would take care of things. It occurred to me that as the last in his family to mind this land, Virgil's responsibility to do the right thing went back 150 years. It did not occur to me that Virgil had already decided what to do about his cat.

In an hour we met at the homestead. We leaned back in simple wood chairs. Virgil sifted his beer through white lips, dusting the porch when he moved.

"Well?" he asked me, his brow a bit lower than in the morning. "You kill that cat?"

"Naw, Virg," Butch jumped in. "Found some kills, though. And the den."

I leaned over to ask Virgil if he was going to shoot it now that we knew where it was. He didn't react to Butch's news, though, so I let it go.

"Yeah," was all Virgil said, and he closed his eyes. He lifted his beer arm again, letting the sweetener wash a little more white off his lips. He smiled a little. "I know where he is, Butch." Then we had dinner, talked about and ignored doctor's orders, and spoke no more about Virgil's lion. The cat is protected by the same covenants that keep the desert wild around Virgil's home, and it's a fair trade.

Longbow

Prodigal Nimrod

In a room behind my mountain home, a dim bulb lights the dusty air that's never been conditioned, except by the high desert. Grey grime covers everything more or less, depending on how long it's been in storage. Last year my old hunting duffels were buried the deepest, but it was elk season in New Mexico, and after five faithless years away I was ready to hunt again. I slapped those bags free of dust, opened them like time capsules, and pulled free the tools of the elk hunting trade.

My commitment to elk used to be like a marriage. It was all-consuming. It tolerated no interference. Elk were my passion until my life broke along its fault lines, and divorce came between me, elk, and everything else I knew. But last fall I was ready to return, the Prodigal Nimrod.

After so much time I might have worried whether elk still lived in the timbered paradise I remembered. But the high country wilderness where elk live doesn't change. Once you've been there, those airless slopes bank a fire in your chest that flares in the fall and calls you back. I was feeling that fire. I was ready to return. And I knew those mountains would be there, unspoiled, just the way I remembered them. They had to be.

When Butch Wilks heard I was hunting elk, he showed up at my door by lunchtime. He spilled an armful of maps in my kitchen, scribbled with block letters and excitable punctuation that looked the way Butch talked, like: "*!!TWO BEARS!!*" and; "*++DEEP WALLOW++!*" Butch is fifty, fit and bespectacled, and he speaks in the stiff cadence of the mountain trapper he once was. His hands are torn and white from laying block in houses below the peaks he rarely visits anymore. He works through hunting season, through all the seasons, victim of his work ethic and the poor economy. But he warns me, like Scrooge's Marley, to change while I still have time. In June, between building other peoples' showers, he rattled his chains on my kitchen table.

"Don't get stuck like me. A feller can't work the way you do when there's critters to thump. *Elk* season is comin'!" He emphasized "elk" in a high pitched way that split the word into nearly three syllables: "*Ayalk!*" After two years of Butch's agitation and five years away from the aspens, I had decided to go for his sake, if nothing else, so he brought the maps.

He spread one open and pinned the rolled edges back with mortared hands. "Take them longbows past Tres Piedres," he said, stubbing a starched finger at paper peaks, peering over his bottle-glass lenses. "It's so purty you can't breathe. It don't help that it's at ten thousand feet, every step straight up. I recollect a place you and Miss Karen can set camp."

When Butch spoke about my wife, "Miss Karen," he sounded like he was holding his hat in both hands. He looked down at the floor, even when she wasn't in the room. He loved to talk to her about the joy of the old days, back when he would trap and hunt freely where our mountain house now stood. But at that moment he was agitated, with harsh words to say, so it was good she had stepped away.

"Dang ATVs!" He bit his lip after the outburst, glancing toward the bedroom, worried Karen might have heard him. "Last time I climbed to Tres Piedres I found a fresh dad-gum *ATV* track. I couldn't catch 'em, but not for lack of trying. When you two get up there, just put a bear load in their tires, OK?" This time, Butch gave both "ATV" and "bear" extra syllables.

Outlaw riders are low on Butch's social registry, even lower than Democrats. I promised to think about it. Butch brightened as he traced a trout stream on the map to a meadowed old homestead on the edge of the wilderness. The slopes swept up from that meadow through thick pine, shown by rippling lines of elevation that made my legs ache. "It's a little steep," Butch shrugged, considerably understating the evidence. "But them big boys pack in there tight. Mebbe they feel safe." I didn't doubt it.

Butch warmed to his topic, which sometimes makes him mix up his words in excitement: "Get Miss Karen a bear tag and a fly rod, too—they take the problem ones from down here and drop them off up there. I catch them up to seventeen inches in the San Antonio, but do you know I had one track me and the girls back to the truck last year, and he wouldn't shake loose until we drove off!"

Once I sorted the fish from fur in his sentences, I was glad that Karen was not, at that moment, in the room. Hunting elk was one thing, but camping among state-certified "bad" bears was another. When Karen returned I edited bears out of the story, and she agreed to join me in the wild.

Karen had never hunted the wilderness, but she was muscled and fit and willing. She began training hard in our arroyos for a high country hunt. She ran in the mountains with her longbow, shredding cactus pads with purple-feathered arrows. She downloaded the virtual habits of digital elk from high alpine web sites. She secured permits for

Tres Piedres for the elk rut. I outfitted us with new tents, stoves, and bags that promised us the Ritz in the woods. I was ready, Karen was willing, and Butch was working. It was time to go.

On the way to Tres Piedres I kept one eye on the road and the other on Butch's scribbled maps. We lurched west at "TURN HERE!!!" and lugged uphill at "**FIRE ROAD STARTS!**" It began to rain. Butch's words echoed in the cab: "You gotta ford the San Antonio River, but it'll be *riled* if there's rain. If it's flowing high, open them Chevy doors and let the river run *through* it. I done that one year and got by." The river barely licked our tires at the crossing. It would not be so easy coming home.

The route was a ten mile string of mud holes and hang-ups from the river to "**OLD CABIN**" where the road, such as it was, ended. We stopped to unload. An old rough hewn frame marked the spot. It was roofless and weathered and small trees grew inside the walls. A wood-planked door swung at an odd angle. I ran my hands over the beams, slipping my fingers into the rough chinked joints, trying to tell old fortunes from axe marks in the pine. I wanted to feel something of the old homesteading souls but the dead logs gave me nothing. I pushed my hands back into my pockets, sheepish. A skeleton, I thought, should not be asked to flesh out its own bones.

"Will these tents hold in the storm?" Karen was worried. The valley blackened.

"Not if we don't get them up," I grinned. "Let's set camp on the bosque, near the stream."

A flowered meadow wrapped the cabin like a skirt. Juggernaut slopes rose from three sides of the field. A stream poured into the meadow's far end, then thinned out into pebbled flats below us. Trout waggled by, seeking deeper cover. A bull elk stood high above us in mid-slope cover, whistling storm warnings. The smell of thick weather filled the air. We set up camp fast in the lee of a stand of trees, near the water.

"How bad will it be?" Karen asked. Her coat began to mist.

"We'll be dry." I said. I believed it at the time.

We rigged tarps, lines, and weights to reinforce the shelter, but high mountain rippers had done me in before, no matter the precautions. I kept those collapsed tent and frozen bag stories to myself. We settled in to sleep on thick pads in bags rated thirty degrees warmer than recommended. Experience had taught me what kind of gear to bring. Dark fell like a curtain. The rain began on cue. The blow came on fast.

"Can't we just leave?" Karen whispered. I didn't answer. We were zipped in and buttoned up, and it was too late to do anything but ride it out. A squall took the valley by force and held it. Lightning fired up and down the meadow in a constant fury. Trees were torn from their roots. The tent buckled, but it held. The stream overran its banks and high water surged through our cook station. Sauce pots banged in the swell. The tarps snapped like sails. We sat together through the night, shivering. When the weather finally lay down, so did we.

The storm withdrew and the dawn advanced. We overslept the morning hunt. When I woke it was clear. Beads of rain focused sun through the fly, painting Karen with blue and yellow bubbles. I sat up, uncovered and chilled. Karen slept. I felt for my glasses, mentally easing myself from our warm bed into the cold shower I would get when I crawled through the vestibule.

"Did we survive?" Karen's voice was muffled by the covers.

"We might have lost a few things."

She kept the back of her bag to me.

"I'll make coffee," I bribed.

"Coffee." We had a deal.

The vestibule washed my collar and the backs of my boots.

Outside I stood mostly upright, taking stock of the damage. My coat dripped onto my long johns. Our camp bull stood full in the sun and bugled. I made a fire and coffee and brought Karen a cup.

"I want to sleep in the truck tonight." She was setting the table for a difficult discussion. I didn't bite. Family picnics had not prepared Karen for the wilderness, an empty slate on which any terrible or happy tale can be written. No outcome is ever guaranteed. Karen's problem wasn't the storm, it was the escape hatch. There wasn't one. No Mister Wizard, no Scotty in the mother ship to beam us up if things went wildly wrong. But that is what I love most about wild places. That was why I had returned.

The wilderness lets us live beyond predictability, where responsibility and consequences are inseparable. Sleeping in the truck was not how I saw us living where the wild things are, but I kept it to myself. Karen let it drop. We dressed and stepped out into the light.

Dusk was a long way off. Dawn had left us a soft forest floor for stalking. It was cool enough to chase our camp bull, who was still bugling madly late in the morning. We were wonderfully alone. The road had washed out and locked us in. Every step in any direction was ours for the taking. With our bows in hand and packs full, we climbed into the roadless wild, courting that camp bull and his three octave come-ons until dark.

Over the coming days we stumbled into elk close enough to touch. We took rabbits for the pot and trout for the pan, but lost gophers and grouse and the arrows we sent after them. The rainstorms thickened to snow. We hunkered over hot coffee by a wet fire. We even spent a night in the truck, finally overwhelmed by the power and fury of new storms, and a little afraid of Butch's bears. We were humbled each morning by the history of that homestead, and grateful for the freedom to fail on our own terms. After a week, with the road destroyed, we blazed our own trail out of the wilderness. It seemed fitting.

We can't go home again, Thomas Wolfe wrote. People age and hometowns wither, and nothing is ever the same. But the wilderness is a constant. It advertises a timeless thing and delivers on the promise. It provides a steady backstop to the constant change in fashion and top forty tunes. It grants a warranty that friends and family can't. People leave, but the wilderness remains. After five years of change and loss I wanted something that would always be what I remembered and loved. I found it again in the wilderness.

I had come home, the Prodigal Nimrod.

*When the weather is bad, sometimes fly-fishing is all there is.
Karen Campbell's first trout on a fly rod.*

LONGBOW

Prescription: Buffalo

Part of me had soured before the expiration date and needed carving out. I was taken from my comfortable home to an operating room, marinated with surgical goo, drugged, prepped, and sliced like a turkey. Afterwards I was wheeled off to the recovery room, left to think about whatever it was I had done to deserve such a fate.

For the next two weeks, friends and family fussed about and blocked the view of anything beyond my own feet, making it hard to see the future. Karen tucked and smoothed my linens, pretending with glad conversation and outsized smiles, but she sobbed in the corner when she thought I was asleep.

It seemed unlikely I would live another week, which made the caller from Montana hard to understand. It wasn't the distance, although I was bedded half a continent away. It wasn't that Karen held the phone to my ear—the connection was clear, and my hearing was still good. I was confused by the future tense of the conversation.

"I'm prescribing buffalo," Doctor E. Donnall Thomas said from Montana. "Water buffalo in Australia, a year from now. I know

Karen Campbell practicing for her buffalo hunt. She eventually worked up from this 60# Hummingbird bow to her 70# (at her 29" draw) O.L. Adcock custom-made longbow after a year.

you won't go without Karen, so if you get well, and get her truly ready to hunt buff, I'll guide her myself. Well, what do you say?"

The thought that I might live another year, let alone that I might ever hunt again, washed me like a spring rain. I said yes without asking Karen. My spirit jumped, as Doctor Thomas knew it would, from the dry white sheets of my hospital bed to the wet green bush of the Tiwi Islands—Australia's buffalo islands.

The Asiatic water buffalo, *Bubalus bubalis*, is 2,400 pounds of perpetually disgruntled bovine. He is aggressively armored under the largest horns of any beast in his genre. He shares overlapping ribs and massive leg and shoulder bones with the Cape buffalo, but he is a larger, harder beast than his African cousin. As Karen cradled the phone, I began planning for her to do something that no woman had ever done, to our knowledge—take *Bubalus bubalis* with a longbow.

I listed our liabilities and assets. To the negative, Karen had been shooting a bow for only a year, and had been hunting twice. To the positive, she was strong, motivated, a black belt with twenty year's experience, and—most importantly—she said she could do it. "It" was stalking to within fifteen yards of a water buffalo on the ground, pulling a longbow to seventy pounds, and sending a one thousand grain broadhead arrow through the animal's vitals. We had a year to prepare.

At the time Karen could shoot a fifty pound longbow well, which is impressive for a woman, to be sure. But the learning curve in archery from fifty pounds to seventy is not linear. The degree of difficulty increases exponentially with each pound of pull. Her limited hunting experience was a further challenge. To help, friends made room for us on the legendary Woodson Lease in central Florida. Karen would stalk deer, pigs, and turkey for the next twelve months, pretending them to be buffalo. I carried my own longbow behind her in the field, walking my way back to hunting strength. She would not be alone in Australia.

O. L. Adcock is a bow maker in southern New Mexico. At the time, there was a five year waiting list for his longbows. The Adcock design had set world records for distance shooting, and I hoped it would give Karen extra power for *Bubalus*. For water buffalo, even seventy pounds is light. O. L. made time for Karen in Roswell, and over lunch he promised her a custom bow in time for her hunt. Owner Ken Beck at Black Widow Bows did the same for me with a PLX eighty-pound longbow. They showed great kindness.

Karen hunted pigs, deer, turkey, Barbary sheep, jackrabbits, and even silver carp while we waited. She crawled every type of terrain stalking beasts from Florida to New Mexico, thinking only of buffalo. Delivery trucks dropped ever-heavier bows at our doorstep until her

Adcock bow arrived. She shot two hundred arrows a day on our desert range. Few arrow makers had the one thousand grain shafts necessary for buffalo, so I designed and built ours using data from the big game broadhead penetration tables of Dr. Ed Ashby. Our 1020 grain carbon laminated arrows hit (and flew) like rebar, breaking through three-quarter-inch plywood easily when tipped with old-school, two-blade steel broadheads.

Tempus Fugit—time escaped. Slowly, my strength came back. Gradually, Karen was able to pull her seventy pound bow one hundred times a day. Suddenly, the year was over and it was July again—buffalo season. We flew to the Tiwi Islands. From New Mexico through Los Angeles, then from Sydney to Darwin, we gained a day when we roared to a stop on Melville Island in Australia's Northwest Territories. It was

Karen Campbell and the author with Karen's water buffalo on Australia's Melville Island. Taken on the ground with one 1120 grain arrow and a STOS two-blade broadhead. Photo by E. Donnall Thomas, Jr.

winter down under. Summer monsoons had passed and the red ruts they call roads were dry and almost navigable.

Winter or summer, Melville Island is hot. The steamy island ecosystem feeds riverine forests of eucalyptus and mellalucca, edged with thick grassland and mangrove swamp. Smoke rifts through the forest from Aboriginal fires set to burn back the jungle. When the bush breaks out onto grey sand ocean beaches, blue pools teem with white sharks and salties (man-eating crocodiles). Brown snakes, green ants, and red spiders make every step dangerous. It is a truly wild place.

The Milikapiti airstrip on Melville Island ended at an open-walled hut tagged with Aboriginal designs. A windsock waved, the limit of local technology. Guide Brad Kane was waiting to drive us four more hours across the empty island to a camp on the Johnson River. The drive was made slower by cow and baby buffalo lumbering across the trail. Brad stopped and taught us buffalo lore with each new animal—how they reacted at a distance and how that changed when you entered their danger zone. We learned what the stalk might be like.

The "Buffalo Stare" - like Satan looking down his nose in judgment - conveys a bull's intensity. The higher the nostrils and the more wildly his eyes roll back to look down that enormous muzzle, the more concern there is that a bull will charge. The stare lasts forever as far as a cramped and frozen hunter is concerned. Thirty minutes to an hour is common. Buffalo rule the island. Buffalo have time. Nothing can rush the torturous review of your every twitch and ruffle. Under direct, close-order inspection, frozen muscles cramp, blood turns to sludge, nerves atrophy, and feet go numb. Brad showed us the basics, although with small animals. Adult bulls would be another story.

"When the big devil stares at you, freeze," Brad said to Karen, although in his bushman accent "stares" and "freeze" came out "*staize*" and "*fraize*." "Don't make a move." Of course, this begged Karen's question. "What happens if we do?" Brad smiled as Aussies always seem to do when they're most serious, and looked up from under his bush hat. "Then," he said, "things get interesting."

We drove into camp at dusk and found Doctor Thomas straddling fresh crocodile tracks on the river, happily fly-fishing for Barramundi. His hair and clothes were wild and he hugged Karen and backslapped me, glad to see our fresh faces and hear news from home after a month in the bush.

No woman had ever been in camp, and Brad put Karen through more of a review than guides usually do. She bested the boys on the range, which settled things down until morning. But we woke early expecting to hunt while Brad had other ideas. "You don't nock an arrow today, either of you." Brad instructed over breakfast. "Not even a thought about shooting today. We'll find a stalk and see how you go." It seemed like hard treatment, but I didn't argue. Brad and Dan Smith, our second guide, had excellent reputations.

At noon we had humped five hard miles and seen neither buffalo nor buffalo sign. That seemed to be an accomplishment on an island packed with five thousand or so wild head. Brad's GPS took us back to the truck where we ate a boxed lunch. Afterwards, we waded along a thin stream, bouncing from wallow to wallow toward the ocean. I was wobbly in the heat, wondering if I had pushed too hard. Then Brad waved us all down thigh-deep in muddy water. "*Freeze!*" he shushed.

We found ourselves crouching three yards from a mountain of gray meat snoring in a wallow. There was nothing to see but the rumbling belly and slumbering sides of a massive buffalo bull.

"Have a go," Brad whispered.

I pushed Karen forward with my free hand.

"Wait!" Brad said, a little sheepishly. "I need to put a pill in me gun first." He slid a finger-sized cartridge out of his breast pocket into the open breach, but when the bolt locked shut the buffalo stirred and stood.

The three of us huddled together looking up at his chest, the head and horns looming as we crouched low in the water. The air was thick with the smell of him.

After an eternity, the bull lumbered away into a bigger wallow. "Hundred and six inches if he's any," Brad whispered. Apparently that was big. The bull stooped and shoveled mud over his back. His eyes burned red through the black muddy streaks on his muzzle. Water plants swung from the tips of his horns.

I stayed behind while Brad and Karen inched forward. Within a few moments she was nose to muzzle with "Satan," as Brad called him, the biggest buff he had ever seen on the island. At twenty yards Satan froze. With Karen in his sights, Brad now just behind her, he gave them the buffalo stare.

"Not a muscle," Brad whispered, locked in a half-crouch. They kept the same position for thirty minutes. Finally Satan stepped away, satisfied they were no threat. "He did look like the devil, didn't he?" Brad smiled at Karen while she crumpled and lay down, massaging her calves. "Let's have another go."

Karen finished her first day with practice stalks on three bulls that never approached Satan's size. Under orders, she never nocked an arrow.

In the morning Karen was given the all-clear to shoot her bow if the situation required it. We were clear with our guides that we would take shots of twenty yards at most, ensuring the best hit and penetration. Then we split up. Six-foot-five Dan Smith walked me and Don Thomas to the highland forest while Brad hiked Karen and fellow archer Rich King toward the ocean.

Brad pushed Karen from buffalo stare to buffalo stalk until she was finished in her heart. Near the end of the day there was barely any game left in her body. Her bow was limp in her hand. Throughout the day's blistering heat (buffalo don't favor the cool morning and twilight hours as most North American game animals do) her one and two hour stalks each ended with a slanted breeze here, a snapped twig there, or a twitching cheek at the wrong moment. Green ants bit her face and fingers while she froze helpless under a buffalo's stare. They dropped onto her neck from leaves and branches, and bit her in swarms, leaving welts before they crawled off to bite again. "I hate," she said later, "those damned green ants." We all did.

Ten hours into the day, toward dark, a last bull detached himself from his harem and fed closer. It was a good one. When Brad offered the stalk first to Rich King, Karen was elated. She was done, all in, and over it. But Rich turned Brad down. "It's Karen's stalk," he whispered, being truly gallant. It was the one thing Karen didn't want to hear, but she kept her disappointment private, gathered up her bow and pack, and crawled back into the breach behind Brad once more.

He wasn't Satan but a slightly lesser demon. His horns were over ninety inches and his thick body would weigh two thousand pounds. Karen's heart raced as it had with each of the other encounters during the day, but this time the reason was different. "At last," she thought, "the sun is going down and it's almost over." Brad stalked within fifteen yards with Karen drafting behind him. The breeze brought the buffalo's smell to her as she crouched and lifted her leg forward. The bull turned and stared.

"Freeze," Brad insisted.

As Karen's leg cramped, the bull raised his muzzle higher to test the wind. He rolled his eyes back to keep her pinned. Green ants crawled across her face. One stretched itself into her nostril. Another

Prescription: Buffalo

Australian guide Brad "Killer" Kane using a found skull to lure a young buffalo into camera range. Photo by Karen Campbell.

bit her cheek. Twenty years of martial arts concentration let her hold still until the bull dropped his head. She mentally drew a plate-sized sweet spot on his chest, just above the front leg where the ribs gave the lungs and heart the thinnest shield.

"Shoot," Brad pushed.

But when Karen, on her knees, drew to the full seventy pounds, the bull turned its head, pinning her down again. She began to let off the string.

"Shoot!" Brad insisted.

As the sun slipped down, Karen pulled back full and let the arrow fly. The bull exploded, scattering buffalo everywhere. Brad ran after in his stocking feet, trying to keep the bull in sight. Karen ran right behind. They lost him, but Brad scaled a termite mound and glassed for movement. More buffalo scrambled through the bush. Karen thought her buff was gone, but Brad finally found the back of him bedded sixty yards away. They stalked close as the sky blackened, easing within thirty yards.

"He's there," Brad whispered, "but if we push it we might lose him." By now Rich King had joined them. He and Karen glassed the buff's back while Brad studied the possibilities. "We'll mark him and back out," he decided.

Karen's heart sank. Neither of them was sure the hit was fatal, but with the bull bedded Brad thought that he would stay down and die. He could hear its labored breathing.

"It was the longest walk I've ever had." Karen said at supper, sadly pushing rice around her plate. She hadn't seen the arrow strike, and there is no room for error on buffalo.

The creatures on the river were as sleepless as we were. We heard them thrash about until the next morning when we made coffee, still in hunting clothes from the day before. The sun found us in somber single file, following Brad's GPS to where the buff had laid up. He held everyone back as he alone peeked carefully over the brush with the sun behind him.

Brad turned and threw up his thumbs, then waved Karen in with both hands, grinning as if he just struck gold. "She did it!" he shouted, sounding as if he never thought she could. We stood around the buffalo in a circle, watching Karen kneel and pat his massive body, all of us quiet, enjoying her moment. Then she handed out hugs to the boys (some of whom went around in line for seconds) before we all dressed her bull for meat. She had found the killing zone, and the bull died quickly from her one arrow.

Prescription: Buffalo

It was my turn to feel done, all in, and over it. My year of recovery was finished. Later at camp I felt empty, wondering how I would get through the next year, or the one after that. Don Thomas stood beside me, reading my mind.

"When," he asked, writing my next prescription, "can Karen be ready for Africa?"

Longbow

Looking for Mister Goodbear

"They come up here to make babies," he said, not embarrassed in the least. The Reverend Scotty Bennett is not one to confuse piety with prudishness. He is also not one to avoid a lengthy explanation. "The Japanese," he began, putting a sermon in drive as we turned north from Fairbanks, "camp out above the arctic circle at forty below, to make babies blessed by the Aurora Borealis." He lifted his voice above the engine to Karen and me, captives on the front bench of his old F-150. "They conceive in weather that can freeze a match, for only a *chance* to see the northern lights. Most of my hunters won't look up even when the sky's on fire. They're too focused on trophies."

He lamented another sixty miles, then downshifted his voice and his truck past the Yukon River. A cold rain turned to snow, though it was June. With the engine quiet, his words carried. "We lose sight of the hunt when we focus on trophies. We miss what's important." Scotty is not one to waste a strong opinion by keeping it to himself. He opened the truck door and limped away, his bad left leg as stiff as the northern ice.

Karen Campbell and Scotty Bennett glassing for black bear near Alaska's Yukon River.

Three years before, the Healy ice pack snapped Scotty's leg and left him trapped and collapsed on the ice. He was saved by his cell phone, although cell phones are not supposed to work on the Healy. Scotty believes it was God, and not AT&T, who delivered him from the wilderness. He also believes it was God, for reasons he does not yet know, who sent him the trials of Abraham afterwards. He can't walk properly. His left leg is more metal than meat. He lost his carpenter's job and learned to drive gas rigs on the winter ice instead. It's dangerous work, but he runs the northern road on eighteen chained wheels now, where his weak leg can't slow him down.

This trip had Scotty back on his feet in the woods for the first time since that bad day on the Healy ice. His heart wanted adventure but he wasn't sure his leg could take it. My wife Karen had never been to Alaska, although she wanted a gentler place than the one Scotty and I described on the drive north. She came to hunt bears, but she was looking for a Mister Goodbear, something much more like Yogi and Boo-Boo than *Ursus horribilis*. I only wanted to see Scotty and show Karen Alaska, so none of us were looking for the epic struggle that most Alaskan hunts become. Still, we were north of the Yukon, we had bear tags, and we were going to give it our best by-God try.

The Yukon River Bridge separates the far north from the *way* far north. When our overloaded tires clopped onto that wood-planked two-lane span, it signaled the beginning of the hunt, even as we hung over the water. A cow moose lumbered along the bridge as we crossed the river, outpacing us easily before she plowed into the thick spruce boughs along the edges. Rabbits bounced on the roadbed and ravens huddled over roadkill. Marmots and chipmunks warmed themselves on the gravel, licking chum from between the stones. Every rise was cluttered with mammals, except bears. Black and brown bruins should have been lumbering about, browsing and digging for early spring food to get their systems moving after hibernation. We saw not a one.

We glassed for bears up and down the Dalton, with the Alyeska oil pipeline at our side. The pipeline and the road twist together through the tundra like a strand of outsized DNA, all the way to Prudhoe Bay. Every few miles we stopped and hiked from the highway to the pipeline through rolling miles of prime bear country. No bears showed.

In the Alaskan summer, hunting is limited by stamina, not sunlight. The sun never sets in early June, so we hunted bears around the clock. We hiked until 2:00 am, until we had to sleep, strange as it was to lie down in good light. For Karen's peace of mind, Scotty had arranged bear-proof beds at the Hot Spot Café, the only rentable space near the Yukon River. Miss Theresa keeps the Hot Spot going in rough country with a raucous, happy hand. She was glad to have Karen's company,

Karen was glad to have hot water, and I was glad Scotty wasn't cooking.

After three days we had seen tracks and scat, but not the bears that left them. We were just too early. The bears were socked in. It was time to look in another direction for our fun, and when we lowered our eyes from the horizon to the roadbed, opportunity hopped. The bushy edges at our feet were crammed with glowing ears and twitching whiskers. The woods were alive with small game. Spring was late, the browse was frozen, and bears were still, but rabbits were everywhere.

After hundreds of empty miles glassing for bruins, the Reverend proposed that we trade bears for hares. Hares in northern Alaska were everywhere the bears were not. Scotty parked, we voted, and it was unanimous - we would hunt *wabbits*, and bears be damned. The big game was off and the small game was on. A mile down the road an arctic hare raised up on thick hind feet, his whiskers glowing, lit from behind by the low midnight sun. Karen stepped to the side of the road and delivered the news bluntly: our hare hunt was afoot.

Rabbit trophies are hard to measure unless action and fun weigh heavy on the scale. The Reverend has always preached that fun is the most important element in any hunt, and he was just as happy - maybe happier - hunting bunnies as bruins. I didn't need much convincing. Scotty and I have never yet let trophies interrupt a good adventure in Alaska. On the Dalton Highway we've almost drowned, chased and been chased by bears, been buried in our tents, and nearly frozen floating caribou meat across a river. We have always had fun, the two of us, our game tags incidental to the expeditions. Hunting, the Reverend Bennett reminds me, is a journey, not a destination.

Every quarry needs special gear, even rabbits. We didn't have store-bought blunts but Scotty made a dozen old school heads in a minute. The Reverend's favorite is a field point with a .38 special brass bullet casing forced over the tip. The design proved effective and economical.

The wide, flat .38 caliber casings knocked the hop out of rabbits from the Yukon River to the Arctic Circle. With Leatherman pliers the heads were easily converted back to target duty after the hunt, making them an elegant, simple small-game solution. I carry a handful of .38 caliber shell casings in my tackle bag now for just such occasions.

Rabbit terminology is often interchanged, but the arctic hare is really its own bunny. It's similar to but not the same as the other *Lagomorphs* that rumpus around the lower forty-eight. The differences don't amount to much: some bunnies are called hares but are rabbits (the Belgian hare), while some are called rabbits but are hares (the jackrabbit). *Lepus arcticus*, the arctic hare, gets its taxonomy right, even if we don't. He is a big boy, averaging twelve pounds, with fat furry Frodo-like feet on which he will stand, bound, buck, kick, lope, run, or leap. He will even use his front fists to box like a kangaroo. Go figure. White in the winter, ours were mottled brown-gray, perfectly hidden until the sun ratted them out from behind, lighting up their thin ears like flares.

What we missed in bears we made up in hares, squared. They bellied up to the roadbed as if it was a bunny bar. Mating season was on, and the competition was fierce and furry. They fought and flirted wildly. Males stood and boxed, and threw their bodies at one another in combat. Females stood to the side while the boys circled around to watch. All of this gave us a target-rich environment, but bringing a bunny down is not all that simple: they are wary, fast, and smart - even when distracted by lust.

We learned to wait a safe distance before we approached on foot. The show was so entertaining that at times we held back to watch. When we did move, we learned that every big game stalking trick is just as important for arctic hares. They are strung tighter than a Steinway. They will sit frozen until the last possible moment, then deploy high-speed escapes early and often. Bunnies are Olympic-class string jumpers, and are often two feet away from an arrow when it arrives, but it was great fun to try. We teamed up on stalks, converged from different directions, and even loosed arrows together, as if we were archers at Agincourt. Fast as they were to run they braked just as quickly, giving us many shots at the same target.

We laughed out loud deep in the timber. Scotty loosened his bad leg on longer hikes, carrying heavier loads. Karen picked her way through the thick spruce after plucky rabbits, and learned to be comfortable alone in the northern woods. We kept sight of what was important. We had fun.

We loosed hundreds of arrows. Most were near-misses, but none caused heartbreak or disappointment. There was always another hare in the hutch, another chance to make up for a close miss. We gave out long before the rabbits did, with bunnies out around the clock.

While we were hunting bears, bears were often hunting for food, scaring unwary bathroom patrons. Note the .475 Linebaugh pistol. Photo by Karen Campbell.

When we left for home the spring thaw came, and black bears multiplied like ... well ... rabbits. One old boar stopped for lunch at the Hot Spot, where he challenged Ms. Theresa's truckers for a teriyaki burger. As Scotty wrote in an e-mail shortly after we left: "The bear made four bluff charges on the bun before a lesson in table manners proved fatal."

I would like to have seen that. I would like to have seen black bears on the tundra thick as buffalo. But life gives us what we need more than it gives us what we want. Scotty needed to know he could hunt on his gimpy leg without leaving us all stranded. Karen needed to know a kinder, gentler Alaska before she plunged into the back country after big bears. I needed to know that my old friend was healed and my wife felt safe.

We all wanted Mister Goodbear, or thought we did, but Alaska gave us what we needed instead. In the end, Alaska gave us what was important, and what was important wasn't a bear at all.

Not this year.

Longbow

Lady Gator

In the proud redneck river country of central Florida, Chris Horsman's big South African voice seemed out of place. His accent clipped the midnight air as he steadied the rocking edge of his airboat. "Take the gator's jaw in your left hand," he instructed my wife, Karen. She didn't move, so he revised the plan. "Maybe I should gaff him then." In hindsight, this was a better approach.

When the steel hook touched the gator's jaw it spun its head in a snap-toothed twist toward Karen's fingers, spraying black water over the boat lights. Chris pinned the gator underfoot as Karen examined her hands, glad to see them still attached. Then she taped the gator's jaw shut, took the gaff from Chris, and lurched the eight-foot lizard into the boat. She sat and rested, breathless and happy in the warm river mist. It was two in the morning, and Karen had taken her first alligator.

I breathed a sigh myself. I was glad it was over, glad I didn't have to dive along a tight line in the dark to drag up a sunken gator, glad that Karen's bow and reel and harpoon held true, and that she was safe and happy. I had suffered during the planning for this trip, afraid of a bad midnight run, dogged by nightmares of my wife being pulled from the boat by a big gator, Ahab-style. Call me Ishmael, but I had been worried for months.

We had booked with Chris a year before, shortly after I learned that sensible gator weapons of choice—an eight gauge shotgun perhaps, or a respectable big bore rifle like a .505 Gibbs—were not allowed on public land. The only weapon approved was a harpoon. We fitted Karen with a bow and arrow with a harpoon head as required by law. But using a harpoon raised the probability—actually the certainty—that any alligator my wife hooked would be alive and extra-feisty when she pulled it to the boat. This gator factoid had me testing tactics for months until the day our guide launched the airboat.

An alligator guide is essential to a hunt in Florida. Chris Horsman is one of the best. He runs a small, personalized operation, perfect for Karen and me as first time gator hunters. He has taken over one thousand gators in his years as a nuisance trapper and guide, many from his airboat on the Kissimmee River in central Florida. When his family was pushed out of Rhodesia (now Zimbabwe) by the Mugabe regime twenty-five years ago, he settled in the states after British military service in the Gulf. He is a big man with a big heart that he wears on his sleeve. I met him volunteering for the Boggy Creek charity camp where he helps kids with cancer have a Florida vacation.

Karen wanted an alligator. Chris guaranteed her safety. That was my only requirement, so we booked the trip. My wife had hunted dangerous game on the ground before but she knew only one thing about alligators: they made her nervous.

She has company. Alligators have invaded the collective American consciousness of fearsome predators, squeezed in alongside great white sharks and flesh-eating bacteria. They belong to a group of night terrors that scare most of us silly. Gators don't have the redeeming cuddly qualities of brown and black bears - they don't play tag or stand up

*Gators are on the move in mating season, and a bit cranky.
Photo by "Alligator Don" Davis.*

on their hind legs to scratch their backs. No. Alligators, like crocodiles and sharks, occupy a fearful primal space in the human cortex. Just their mention produces a sphincter twitch and a shudder. In the south they are numerous and multiply quickly.

Alligators, caimans, and crocodiles are cousins, part of a crocodilian family tree which has barely branched since the Jurassic age. Crocodiles worldwide are voracious man-eaters, responsible for perhaps three thousand deaths yearly. The American alligator (*Alligator mississippiensis*) however, is more manageable and much smaller. Crocodiles may reach over twenty feet while alligators rarely exceed fourteen feet in the wild, and even the very large gators rarely attack humans. In the last forty years there have been about twenty fatal attacks reported in the United States. Bees kill more people.

Children, dogs, and drunks in fresh water are most vulnerable to attack by these opportunistic omnivores. Yet gators are generally tolerant of humans, a factor in their near-extinction from over-hunting in the mid-twentieth century. As a result, alligators were classified as "endangered" until 1987, when their status was changed to "threatened," largely due to their resemblance to the American crocodile. Floridians, who saw the population explode to over one million gators in 2008, are not sure any protection is needed. Every central and south Florida golf course pond and drainage ditch seems to hold a resident reptile, and complaints of nuisance gators grow exponentially.

Even so, the protection for alligators is strict. Limited hunting is allowed but only through a system of trapper's licenses, restricted to certain areas. Trappers must apply for and be granted permits, although they are allowed to use "agents" to assist in taking gators. Karen was using an agent permit to take her alligator. I was along as the photographer.

If gators are relatively harmless to the general public, all bets are off when a live gator is pulled to the boat. My concern for Karen's safety was well-founded, and I wanted her to have the best gear possible for the hunt. I needed a bow, a reel, a harpoon arrow with an alligator head, and a float.

Bows today come in old-fashioned and modern forms. Alligator hunters may choose from Robin Hood-style longbows, Olympic-style recurves, or modern, cam-geared compound bows. Traditional archers and modern compound bow shooters often argue the relative merits of their equipment for hunting. However, both camps usually agree that for alligator hunting, either style works equally well. Karen shoots a heavy bow so I modified a high-tech fifty-six pound longbow into a take-down, and matched it to a very modern bowfishing reel. Line flows from the reel to a bow-mounted detachable float so an alligator won't end up tied to you and your bow. I replaced the standard two-hundred-pound test line with six-hundred-pound gator cord, and attached the reel and the float to the bow with strap-on gadget adapters. All that was left was to choose the arrow and point, and practice with the gear. Muzzy makes tough bowfishing arrows and a beefy "gator" head with a heavy-duty harpoon flange to fasten the arrow into the alligator. I had tested a number of reel and arrow/point combinations on carp during the summer, and I was sold on these arrows and the AMS "slide" device that always keeps the line in front of the bow. It avoids a dangerous tangle. Karen had practiced on carp as well, so after an afternoon in the back yard dialing in a ten-yard shot (those heavy arrows drop quickly past ten yards), we were ready.

In central Florida, spring, summer, and fall blend into one long sultry season that stretches from March through November. The heat keeps the cold-blooded alligators moving late into the year. Karen was sweaty in the sheen of a hot September night when we met Chris and his friend Bill Teat at sunset. We were near the little town of Yeehaw Junction, and the name of the town fit my mood perfectly. I was fired up for the all-night hunt ahead of us, even if Karen was focused and not quite as bubbly. She was the shooter after all, with all the obligations and responsibility. I was just along for the ride.

Karen had begun hunting only three years before, but had learned hunting tactics with small game, wild pigs and water buffalo. She was beating the learning curve by traveling around the world, facing new challenges every few months. She was comfortable on the ground, but we were putting her on the water. She would have to hit her mark with new gear from a rocking boat. She worried about big things in the black water outside our halo of lights, things that could do us harm. She worried about hooking a lizard nearly as long as the boat. But when Chris launched our airboat on the Kissimmee River, she worried only about surviving the ride.

Ride a lawnmower down a water flume through a gator pond and you'll understand airboats. The lawnmower ride will be quieter, more stable, and safer than an airboat, but you'll get the idea. As Chris gunned the propeller Karen and I huddled in the front, whipped by muck and mosquitoes, unable to focus on the gators flashing by. We were wrapped in safety goggles and earmuffs, chilly even in the steamy September night as Chris raced downstream. Bill pointed to gators zipping by, some holding their mouths open, others swimming toward or away from us, all with their eyes glowing bright from the boat lamps. But we were deaf, dumb, and blinded by the ride. We could not tune in fast enough to absorb it all. Conversation was out of the question.

It was the gators' eyes that necessitated a night hunt. Alligators hang in the water with their heads barely breaking the surface, almost impossible to see. But in the dark their eyes reflect a spotlight and give their position away. Chris took us downstream fast through the Kissimmee River locks, then cut the engine and swept the water with a single spot. The surface sparkled with alligator eyes. Thirty pairs of red reflectors lit the river along the yellow beam. It almost seemed we could walk across the Kissimmee on gatorback. But seeing gators and taking gators are very different things.

We floated quietly down a wide stretch of river. Karen had recovered from the high-speed ride and happily took her place on the flat forward deck, bow and reel in one hand, the other pulling tension on the string and harpoon. Bill sat nearby to give instruction. The trick wasn't getting close enough to a gator but getting close to a gator that was big enough. Four and five footers were young and curious and let us near, but Chris wanted a big animal for Karen, at least eight feet long.

For her part, Karen was ready to shoot any lizard in range when Chris gave the order, no matter the size.

And so we settled in to the hunt, floating, quiet, occasionally motoring to a new spot, always looking for a pair of eyes with enough skull between them to announce a quality gator. All hunters know these long quiet stretches that test our patience. Whether we are camped on a stand, crammed into a blind, or sitting in the woods, we expect to spend long hours waiting for the flash of animal action that comes and goes so quickly. But on the Kissimmee the sheer number of alligators made the wait exciting. Minutes, then hours ticked by as Karen kept tension on the string. Four pairs of eyes on the boat scanned hundreds of red-eyed heads below the hull. Again and again Karen came to full draw over small gators, only to have Chris stand her down, jerking the light from the gator's back as he took its full measure.

When Karen's arms needed a break Chris gunned the boat ashore in an oxbow. He tried a predator call, but more for our amusement than any hope of success—there were no takers. Both our guides spent time in the dark sharing stories of big gators that dive deep and die on the bottom after being hit, of diving along the tight line and feeling for the lizard in the dark, slipping a loop around the body to pull it up. It appealed to me to try it in some alien-experience way, but Karen waved me off the idea as sharply as Chris had waved her off the small gators.

At one in the morning, Bill steadied Karen's back with one hand, and pointed into the night with the other. "Get ready" he whispered, though she had been stuck on ready for hours. The boat floated on a collision course with a big lizard swimming into range. "Shoot!" Chris called out, as Karen raised her tired arms and fired a harpoon under the water, just behind the gator's head. He was five yards away at the shot. "You hit him!" Chris shouted, his accent seeming less out of place in the excitement. The line jerked tight and the alligator sank below and behind the boat, stripping off the cord slowly. Karen cleared more line for a float-popping run that never came. It was quiet as we waited, listening to water gently lap the sides of the hull.

"Is he on?" Chris called quietly from the pilot bench above as he climbed down to help. I handed Karen a second fully-rigged bow and put her first one aside. She readied herself to shoot again. The line was tight but quiet.

"I don't know if he's on," Chris said.

But as he pulled the dead weight of the line hand over hand, he cried, "He's on!" The lizard came into view slowly, up through the black water, the harpoon perfectly fixed behind the head. His open eyes broke the surface above a long body hanging deep into the river.

"Great shot!" Bill said, backing out of the way for Karen to put another arrow in the gator. But it didn't move, and seemed to be dead. "I've never had one die so fast," Chris said, surprised.

During the night our guides had shared stories of "dead" alligators that had revived in the boat on the way back to camp, clearing the decks and scattering hunters into the water. Chris had long ago adopted a bang stick policy for gators in the boat—his "dead gator" rule—but he had suspended it reluctantly for us. Karen wanted to use only a bow and a knife. When Chris suggested that she clamp the gator's jaw shut with her hands, I made loud "no" noises in my head while Karen held back, which proved to be a good thing. Her gator—not a monster, but a respectable eight footer—snapped back to life and thrashed and bit when Chris brought the gaff near its mouth. Karen wrapped its jaw shut with tape.

We rested after Karen hauled the gator aboard. "Nice work," Chris said. "Yeah," Bill echoed, "Really nice work," upping the ante for compliments. I didn't have the words or the energy to compete, so I

Karen Campbell packed her own alligator from the boat the old fashioned way - on her back.

kept my thoughts to myself and proudly handed my wife a knife instead. She ensured that the gator was more than "mostly" dead for the ride home, and Chris was at ease at last.

The night took my breath and my words away, but I was the proudest and most relieved man on the boat. I was looking forward to a gentle ride home in the early light, on a river and a boat which seemed much tamer than the night before, sitting next to a woman who seemed much wilder. After a long night of worries and waiting, Chris swung the boat back toward Yeehaw Junction, and the little town with a hollerin' name fit my mood perfectly once again.

Jukebox

Jukebox had been seen on and off for ten years on our ranch, a span of sightings which, if confirmed, would have extended his life well beyond the laws of nature. But just as belief must sometimes bend to fact, fact must sometimes bend to belief, and our belief in Jukebox was strong, even if he was only a turkey.

But to suggest that Jukebox was "only a turkey" on our Florida lease would have been a sin greater than questioning the Gators' prospects for a decade of national titles. The offending member would have been cast out of our hunting paradise without possibility of probation or appeal. I say "would have been" because, to my knowledge, no one had ever been foolish enough to question the existence of Jukebox, not out loud.

Jukebox was first revealed to Craig Courty in the Airplane Hammock, the last stand of black cypress in the furthest reaches of our ranch. It was a dark circle of swamp wrapped by a wall of blackberry bush and Sawtooth Palmetto, a warp of thorns and weft of spears woven taller than a man and ten yards wide. Whether Jukebox chose Mister Courty or the other way around, neither could have set a better stage for the encounter than that deep pocket. Gators swam the bottom. Buzzards coursed the top. And it was haunted.

The wreck of a World War II trainer still littered the bottom, as it had since the plane and pilot were lost during the second of our wars to end all wars. The violence of that long-ago implosion hung in there like the echo of a holler. It led to sightings and thoughts that kept most folks away, but not Craig Courty. The Airplane Hammock may have been a ripe place for hallucination, but it was a haven for deer and turkey.

The morning he met Jukebox, Craig quit the field early. He slipped back to camp alone. He set his shotgun down softly, as if he might not raise it again. He cooked the camp breakfast, but kept his usual blare of tasteless disco to a respectful volume. His morning bracer

Big Boss turkeys like this Osecola Tom in Florida were half the size of Jukebox.

stayed corked. Folks drifted in from the woods and took their seats, drawn by his hot bacon biscuits but quieted by his dark mood. He was humble and hushed and so out of sorts that no one spoke, except to ask for butter.

"I saw *Him*, boys," he finally said, and pushed his eggs across the plate. "I was backed up to a cypress, camo from head to toe. I was covered so good I couldn't make out my own feet. I gave a little cackle, that's all. He slipped up behind me in the fog and I never heard him coming." Then he paused, eyes wide behind coke-bottle glasses, and whispered: "*But I felt his footsteps.*" A few members slowed their breakfast.

"I cut my eyes around and almost swallowed my call. I had to look up to see him." Craig is six foot three, and seems taller sitting down. His description began to gain traction. "I thought it was a cow at first. His beard was long as a calf's tail. It would have swept the ground, but he was too tall." Forks froze in mid-shovel. "His wattles popped up off his neck like red, white, and blue balloons in July." Craig's voice rose, his hands spread wide in the air as if he were measuring a blue whale. "And when the sun lit him through the trees, he glowed like" and here Craig lowered his voice to a reverent hush, "*Old Glory.*" With that, breakfast stopped.

Craig Courty was patriotic to a fault. For him to compare a bird's neck to the American flag was a life-altering event. Folks stopped wolfing his cheese and garlic grits, a considerable achievement in itself. His lip trembled. "I thought I had him, boys, but he looked through me like he could see my soul." Craig's shoulders slumped, and then he confessed: "I never even raised my gun." Strong men looked away.

His chin fell. He might have slumped further, but all the sag in him was used up. "I've been hunting here since I was nine years old, and I never saw anything like him," he said. "Hell, I never even *heard* of anything like him." Then he clamped his hat to his head with both hands and exhaled, "That bird was as big and bright as a danged, well, a danged *Jukebox*!"

And there it was. Craig was so chastened that his friends were sure of only one thing: Whether this mutant boss tom turkey was real or not, Craig Courty believed he was real, and that counted for a great deal. "Jukebox," the members murmured, and so it began.

There was speculation through the day that Jukebox might be an outright invention. After all, Craig was known to sidestep facts that might inconvenience a story. But the chance that a bird of such outsized dimensions might be real was too great to ignore.

That night folks yawned and made excuses to retire early, and suggested that in the morning they might hunt the oak bottoms to the north or west. But before dawn the eastern road to the Hammock was gridlocked with swamp buggies as members jockeyed for position. Before light each tree hid a man in a camouflaged pod of some sort, ready to open deadly fire. As the sun rose, fifteen painted faces searched out the monster Craig reported. And they were rewarded, if the encounter could properly be called a reward.

That morning Jukebox thundered in the distance. He hammered the early air. His gobbles exploded in strings, each pounding out before the echo of the last one died. He stormed the hammock at dawn and eyeballed every hunter in his hide. He seemed to block the sun and shake the earth. He was blinding blue and crimson in one moment, ghostly grey and invisible in the next.

In sum, Jukebox was a showcase of such overwhelming extravagance that for the first time in Craig Courty's life, exaggeration had failed him. He had told the truth. But talking about Jukebox and taking Jukebox proved to be very different propositions. That first day the members were stunned into submission. No one even raised a gun.

JUKEBOX

Jukebox showed again that year, and for years thereafter. He was never at risk. Those who crossed him were marked forever. "You don't hunt Jukebox," men said, "He hunts you." On such days a troubled man would later sit at his breakfast, humbled by the bird who spurred boss toms bloody and seeded hens by the score. His body drew the expletives men usually reserve for centerfolds and monster trucks. He froze men senseless with a stare. In ten years no one ever fired a shot.

When I joined the ranch, Jukebox had already lived twice the lifespan of an Osceola tom. The trail to his hammock had been abandoned. He was real but unreachable, like the surface of the sun or Angelina Jolie. He had become a fixture on the ranch, as rooted and essential as the oaks. Men spoke of Jukebox, but they no longer dreamed of taking him.

I knew nothing of turkeys, but I wanted the King of Birds. I bought every tomfool trick the stores would sell me: box, blow, and scrape calls; fixed, folded, and power decoys; pop, drape, and drag-in blinds. I jumped into turkey hunting expecting the success I had known hunting other animals in other places, but I was never a threat to Jukebox. My new campmates watched me with quiet tolerance. I was no threat to any bird.

Four weeks of hunting passed painfully, like bad Texas chile. The calls, blinds, and decoys I purchased left me flat. On the last day of the season I sat in the dark, defeated. My interest had long since wandered from Jukebox to any fool jake that might come near my killing zone. But no bird had come close enough to take with any weapon, let alone the bow I carried.

"It would be a shame," my friend Chip said before the season, "if you take a turkey your first year." I raised an eyebrow. He continued. "Early success only encourages the wrong sort of people to hunt." It occurred to me that I might be the wrong sort of person he was referring to. "Failure, on the other hand," he wrapped up, "is good. Failure builds character." Character was all I could hope for. But there were six hours left in the season, and I had nothing to lose.

I left my blind for that inner circle of hell where Jukebox lived. I cut my way into the Airplane Hammock. Vines raked my belly. Thorns ran me through. I waded on, calling for Jukebox until the wreck of that World War trainer stopped me cold. Broken cables breached the surface, reaching up from the wreck below. I stood shivering, chilled to the bone. I wanted Jukebox, but I settled for warmth.

The swamp brightened in the new sun as I turned to go. Airplants flowered. Crimson blooms colored the trees like Christmas. I picked one for my wife, consolation for our lost season. I wiggled out the way I had crawled in, dragging my bow in one hand and Karen's flowers in the other. The sun blinded me. I lay in the grass, warm but teary. I soaked up heat. I was ready for bed.

When my eyes cleared, the largest turkey I had ever seen stood twenty steps away. There was no mistaking Jukebox, even in old age. But ten long years had ravaged his body. His once massive back swayed under its own weight. His legs buckled. His wattles had gone grey. The skin on his neck hung like an old suit, and thin quills poked from bare patches where feathers used to pop and shake. He seemed nearly blind, squinting through watery lids. When he finally saw me he was shocked, flat footed in surprise. So was I.

He waddled toward the hammock by the most direct route, no matter that I was in the way. He gained speed. It seemed he might fly, but his mass argued against it. I dropped the flowers. I had a vision of him mounted in my den, preserved in his youth. He ran faster. I slipped an arrow free. Success was certain. I pulled my bow up only to feel greenbriars lashing it down. I was frantic, jerking with both hands to loose the limb, my neck craned to watch the bird advance. At fifteen steps the limb ripped free. At ten steps I nocked an arrow. At five steps I drew as he lumbered into the air and sailed safely home. I never even fired a shot.

Jukebox escaped the consequences of his mistake. I carried mine back to camp. Craig Courty stood in his kitchen, a spatula in his left hand, a cigar and morning bracer in his right. Disco blared from the radio. Ten years had been kinder to Craig than to the bird he had named. He cooked and swayed to the music, standing in his plastic pink clogs, happy. He brought me hot garlic grits to trade for the story I had dragged home. "I saw him, Craig. I saw Jukebox." "Do what?" He peppered me with questions. He inquired after the bird as one does a dear friend. Then he sat quiet, lost in thought about the old gobbler who seemed close to death. I shoveled in my breakfast. I was uncomfortable with the silence.

"You might hunt him again, Craig," I offered. "I bet you could take him now that he's lost a step." I wanted the words back before they cleared my lips. Craig stared at me like I had slapped his dog. He leaned in close. "Son," he sighed, "when a turkey is smart enough, and lives long enough to get his own name, there's only one thing you can do." He lit a new cigar and leaned back to exhale before he finished his thought: "You stop hunting him."

Then he stood and filled my plate, happy that Jukebox was still in his world.

Longbow

Got Gator?

Chris Horsman barked in his British/Rhodesian redneck accent, a muddle of language from the three continents he calls home: "Put another arrow in 'im!" Karen slipped on the deck handing me a newly rigged bow, her other arm spilling harpoons and cameras. "He's coming *up!*" Chris warned from the Captain's seat above. His voice broke on the last word. Karen tipped me the new bow from her knees, and pulled back the one I had just fired. White gator cord streamed over the red railing into the night. I leaned into the rail for a second shot as the line stirred the water into a boil. "Here he comes!" Chris shouted. The 10 foot gator breached the river and rolled, a long spinning spot for my second shot. I missed. He rolled again, snapped off my first harpoon, and swam past the lights into the night, free of the floats and lines. "Oh bloody hell," Chris muttered.

That phrase was beginning to sound familiar. Those same unhappy words had sputtered out of Karen's cell phone a few hours earlier. "Spare's buggered" and "wrong bloody tire" were the other bits of foreign speech I overheard - the ones I can repeat - as we sped across central Florida. Chris' airboat was broken down on the roadside, and our alligator guide was at the AutoZone sorting out a blown tire. Our sunset airboat launch was on hold.

Karen and I had our own problems. While she drove I rigged bows, reels, and harpoons in the back seat of the truck. Our gator gear was piled beside me where I had thrown it after a movie matinee. The film was a bribe to our kids, who agreed to behave while we raced to this all-night, last-minute, end of season October hunt. As the credits rolled up on "Max Payne," we rolled out to the river. I can't recommend the movie, but the kids were happy. I was not.

Captain Chris Horsman is a big, personable man with a small, personalized business. He guides for gators. He's good at it. Karen had tagged her first gator with him on a mad midnight hunt a week earlier. I was happy about her hunt. I was happy with Chris. But I was unhappy about my gear. Chris had called at the last minute with his last gator tag. My reels were empty and my arrows weren't rigged. I wasn't ready. But if my hunt was like Karen's, I would see hundreds of alligators. All I had to do was hit one, reel it in, and return with ten fingers and two hands. I wasn't ready, but I took the tag. You would have done the same.

In a spotlight at night a gator's eyes shine like wet rubies. Alligator hunting is a vampire-like crocodilian cruise that ends when you fall asleep or at dawn, whichever comes first. We were hunting red eyes on black water with white lights, looking for the wide space between the eyes that means a big gator. Over a million alligators prowl Florida's waters, crowding retention ponds and bass lakes, eating anything that moves. *Alligator mississippiensis* has made a remarkable recovery from endangered status in the mid-twentieth century. But today gators are as common as cowpies, and hunting thins the herd.

Chris finally came to the river with his airboat and his tough old man Pete. Pete is a gator trapper too. He has the added distinction of having survived two rifle rounds to his head during the Mugabe wars in Rhodesia. Eventually Mugabe's thugs took Pete and Chris' home and they moved to England, then America. They survived Rhodesia – many did not. Pete and Chris are hard men: not easily impressed, steady in a fix, and perfectly suited to chasing crocodilians.

They inspected my bow reels and slide devices that keep the line out in front of the arrow at full draw. I had two longbows set up with bow-mounted floats to pop off and follow the gator. The fishing arrows were tipped with harpoon heads. Chris wanted me to rig my line directly to the harpoon instead of to the plastic slide, but there wasn't time to change my set-up. It was a mistake.

Karen held me close as Chris roared off. He sat high in the pilot's seat ahead of the prop. Pete washed the water with light, look-

Author at full draw on his alligator hunt. These hunts always go well-past midnight, and things always seem to go wrong, as they did on this hunt. Photo by Karen Campbell.

ing for the red-eyed glow of a gator. On Karen's hunt there had been hundreds, but for an hour we powered up side creeks, through heavy reed beds and along brushy banks. Nothing. We got no more than a bullfrog's croak for our trouble. Chris finally throttled the prop off. We stopped and floated mid-river, disappointed. Pete quietly worked the light.

"*There's* the bugger!" Pete shouted, twisting the British verb into a noun. Red reflectors danced at the end of his spotlight, a hundred yards away. Chris throttled up the prop and deafened me. I balanced on the forward deck. My harpoon was ready. The deal was simple: Chris would tell me when to shoot on a gator ten feet or better. I turned from Chris to the gator, waiting for a sign. He ignored me and throttled forward until we were almost on top of the lizard, the big boss gator of this part of the river, used to brushing off challengers.

"Shoot, *cripes*, shoot!" Chris's shout pushed through the prop noise. I drew three inches past my normal anchor, leaned over the rail, and released the harpoon. White cord played out in the air behind the arrow. The shaft sank in with a thunk, and line piled up on the gator's back. His spiked tail flipped up and he came at the boat. "You hit him good!" Chris shouted out. The gator dove under the boat, stripping the reel. I stood there useless, but Chris barked me back to action. I had prepared for this. I had another bow rigged with a reel, float, and harpoon for a quick second shot. Karen handed it to me. The gator plowed to the surface. Chris' shouts drowned in the prop wash. Everything went according to plan. Until I missed.

That, I hadn't planned on.

When the gator broke free I stood alone in the dark with a pounding head, two empty reels and no gator. *Oh Bloody Hell*, I thought, sounding to myself just like Chris, who was already pointing out my poor aim and arrow set-up. He was sure that the plastic slide had fractured and released my gator. So was I. I felt stupid, and I regretted not re-rigging the arrows. When I reeled in the arrow, we were both surprised to see that the solid carbon shaft had snapped in half. The slide held but the arrow failed and released the line. I was still on the hook, even if my gator wasn't. If I had rigged the line to the head, or hit with my second harpoon, I would have been reeling in the gator instead of feeling sorry for myself.

    I pulled the wet mess of lines and floats on deck while Pete and Karen smoothed the knots and I rigged one bow. It took time. Chris stayed above us in the pilot's seat, searching for the gator. The lizard had swum away on the surface, giving us his direction. That proved fatal. Chris watched for bubbles, ripples, wakes or ridges – anything to signal a hiding place. Pete swept the surface with spotlights. We motored along the banks. An hour passed until Chris caught a glint in the willows 100 yards away, a flash off the gator's long ridged back. He throttled forward again until the rippled back and broken shaft were close. When I shot and connected behind its head, the gator boiled out of the willows toward us, towing the float. I hit him with a third harpoon and he dove again, taking the arrows, lines and floats with him. He was gone.

    The propeller sputtered and stopped. It was late. I was tired. A hunter's moon rippled on the water. The boat gently rocked. Karen handed me a broadhead harpoon, one of three remaining. We couldn't rig the arrows, all the line was on the gator. The reels were empty. We sat silent, and no one moved.

    The floats surfaced first, then the big gator. He came up in the shallows beside the willow roots and rolled. Another harpoon snapped. Only one line held. We drove closer and he swam across the river again. I sent a broadhead through his chest at 15 yards, then another. Bubbles blew into the water. He turned back to the willow bank and buried him-

Author with his 10 foot, twice-found gator, after an all-night hunt of this reptile that seemed immortal. Photo by Karen Campbell.

self there. There was one arrow left. Chris eased the boat to the willows and I drove the last harpoon through.

I thought he was dead. We all did.

I pulled him in by a harpoon and my "dead" gator snapped his head back at my hands, his jaws open. Chris pushed Karen aside and gaffed the mouth shut with a hook. The gator jerked against the gaff as I taped its mouth. He bent the steel hook straight, slid off the gaff under the boat, and was laying on the shallow bottom. Under a spotlight, the tape on his jaw looked tight. Chris and I plunged our arms deep in the water and hauled the gator on board by hand while his tail snapped and he tried to roll. Chris held him down, and I used an old Randall knife to finish the work. The hunt was over.

Or so I thought. We cut free the lines and floats. I salvaged one harpoon, and sat next to my alligator on the deck, rigging my bow again. I was almost afraid it would need another arrow. Then Pete interrupted my thinking, and he made me an offer: "I've still got another tag, my last one. Let's find another gator."

I sat beside my ten foot trophy and looked at the broken shafts and the rips and tears in him from six harpoons. I felt like Ahab. I felt aches in my back and my arms, and I was lucky to have this big gator on the deck. Chris and Pete had found the animal against all odds, using hard work and experience to overcome my mistakes. On the other hand, I knew how to do it right this time, and my bow, reel, and harpoon were all rigged and set to go. I was ready.

I was ready, but I turned down the tag. You would have done the same.

Longbow

Red Sky at Night

Karen stood against a red cotton sky, sorting through the pigs below her by sex and size. Boars and sows milled about in the late warm light. She pointed her longbow at one, then another, and made a hard choice. I sat below in a blind of palmettos, knowing her shot would spark a stampede, and waiting for the quiet that would follow. The sun set as her arrow came to rest. She drew and released as the sky flamed red and then the woods grew still in the dark.

    Karen climbed down. Her boots scraped on the last rung of her stand, then broke through palm fronds and palmettos after her pig. It was a bruiser based on the commotion it made tearing away. Orange trees sweetened the warm night air. I stayed under my low sweep of oaks trying to relax, packing up cameras. But there was work to do, and supper would be ready soon. I stood and joined my wife at the swamp's dark edge. After nearly a year away, it was good to be hunting. It was good to be together. It was good to be in the woods instead of at work.

    It had been a brutal year. I took a job in Wisconsin, a thousand miles from my Florida home. I was in the air more than in my own bed. I was happy for the work, but after nine months away from the woods and my wife, I needed a vacation. I flew home. We went hunting.

Karen and I live on Florida's blue water bikini coast, but we hunt in its dark swampy center. There is no blue water in swamp country, and bikinis should be banned, or at least better regulated. Where we hunt, Central Florida is all about big jeans, mud buggies and bass. The rivers wander more than they run, so most of the land is wet. All of the land is overrun with pigs. When de Soto first freed hogs on a Florida beach in 1539, he couldn't have imagined they would conquer the state before his soldiers did. But wild pigs have become a permanent fixture in every part of the sunshine state. They are smart and fun to chase, but hard to hunt when time is precious.

On our first day back in the woods, every moment felt precious. We scouted pastures and the swamp edges for sign, then set up late in a grove of wet-bottomed oaks. The plan was to ambush pigs on a trail through the oaks from one pasture to another. Karen was on a high stand, I was below with a camera. The sun flattened into the horizon. Shadows stretched into black fingers. Nothing moved. The sky flamed red, and I remembered the old mariner's blessing: *red sky at night, sailor's delight.* I hoped it would apply to us. As the sun set in the west, a ball of squeals and grunts rolled toward us from the east. Dozens of pigs shouldered in between Karen and me, rooting and tossing mud in the air. She took her shot.

"Did you see that big boar, the tusks on him?"

In fact I had been preoccupied with the sunset.

"I wanted that boar. He had his butt to me."

I nodded. I hoped there was not a butt-shot boar in my immediate future.

"I wanted the big boar, but it was getting dark. A big sow turned broadside."

I knew what she would say next.

"I took the sow."

Karen's martial arts background and black belt body made her a natural shot with a bow soon after she took up archery. But shooting isn't hunting. It was her passion for wild places and her acute sense of right and wrong that helped her become a true hunter. Still, it didn't come easily. Nothing worthwhile ever does. In the five years since we married, she has chased big and small game from Alaska to Australia. There have been successes (her water buffalo with a longbow) and setbacks (bears have not been kind to her). But this night, Karen passed up a trophy boar when the shot wasn't right, and showed how far she had come. She was responsible in her choice, and she was happy with the result. At least as happy as a woman can be who hasn't yet found her pig.

"Do you hear that?"

Her sow sighed in the shallows. Karen moved ahead, but I held her back. Wounded pigs are trouble.

"It was a good shot, buried to the feathers, but I can't find any blood."

After casting about where the arrow first struck the pig, neither could I. Our flashlight died faster than the pig. We stood together in the black, listening to hog's breath echo off oaks and water. The distance was hard to guess.

When the sound stopped, Karen went to camp for high boots and bright lights. I walked into the flow of black water to pass the time. I thought about gators. I lifted my leg over a log, but in mid-step it became bristled, bloody, and big. I hoped the beast suddenly between my feet was more than mostly dead, and poked it with my toe. I lowered my leg. Karen's pig was perfectly hit, perfectly dead, and a long muddy drag from the truck.

Karen returned and gave me a hug and a high-five. The mariner's blessing ran through my head again, with a twist: *red sky at night, woman's delight.* The pig was nearly 200 pounds - tough to take with a longbow, and tough to drag through the swamp. Karen had done the hard part, so dragging the pig home was my job.

I was on vacation, but I was happy for the work.

Karen Campbell with a dandy Florida swamp pig, taken just at dark.

Coons, Cuisine, and Counterinsurgency

I am told that Faulkner, the South's most celebrated if long-winded author, favored coon for supper. I imagine him in his Alabama study, stretching sentences into pages, simmering a hind of raccoon to flavor his endless thoughts. I imagine Faulkner eating coons as it is easier than imagining that I am eating one. Despite his celebrity, William F. did not leave a legacy of raccoon on the table in Dixie.

In the south, disagreeable things are often disguised as tolerable meals. This is our redneck reality game, a "Guess What's Coming to Dinner?" culinary contest. But raccoon has never achieved even the passable status of other secondary southern foods like possum, or okra. We're a daring bunch in our kitchens, but we don't eat coon. I consider it only because killing raccoons is a condition of my hunting lease, and I like to eat what I kill, unless it's with my car.

I hunt the green workday savannas between Florida's holiday white beaches, where State Roads 60 and 441 cross and create Yeehaw Junction, an excitably named but otherwise empty intersection. I hunt where Florida, a state more southern in latitude than culture, tolerates a few Cracker traditions of the old south. One of these is the age-old

Coons seem cute and cuddly, like this one in a tree, but they cause great damage to other wildlife.

redneck conflict with *Procyon lotor*, the modern raccoon.

On my land, Jihadist raccoons have escalated that conflict into a full-on furry *fatwah*. They savage our camp. They eat our turkeys. More precisely, they eat our turkeys' eggs. To preserve our Osceola gobblers, my partners and I afford raccoons all lawful due process, then trap, snare, tree, and shoot them when we can. But raccoons are not so easily killed, not by any method. These masked sociopaths are winning our war on coon nation.

Imagine a cat. Imagine the violence involved in dispatching that twisting, vicious kitty if it knew what you were up to. Now imagine that cat twice as smart, three times as large, and four times as mean. Also imagine that your *El Gato Diablo* is gifted with an opposable thumb and

Coons, Cuisine, & Counterinsurgency

delicate fingers, criminal fingers with which it can hack into your computer, or unlatch the safety on your handgun. The raccoon is all of that and more. If the devil liked turkey eggs, the devil would be a raccoon.

And there's the problem: appetite. Raccoons will eat anything. Like wild pigs, tame goats, and other trash-mouthed southern animals, raccoons are omnivores. But of all the edibles in the world, coons like turkey eggs best. Turkey eggs are tasty, easy to find, and they can't run far. Which means that on our lease, coon growth and turkey loss are plotted in startling and opposing trends. As Churchill said of pendants and prepositions, this is a condition up with which we will not put. We leaseholders claim the exclusive right to kill our gobblers. We get upset when raccoons presume to do our business for us. Our double extra-large southern panties get all bound up at the mere thought. So we have decided: on our land, coons must be exterminated, and with extreme prejudice.

Once you start hunting coons, you become convinced they know your thoughts. You are certain they monitor you on the Internet. When trapped they free themselves, and then their friends. When chased they cloak themselves in stealth technology. They dodge every projectile from stone to bullet. Dynamite is effective but frowned upon, even in the south. Unless the old ways are employed: the midnight chase with hounds and horses, smudge pots glowing off pitchforks and flugelhorns sounding through the fog, hunting raccoons is a loser's game of chance. As those old school methods violate other express tenants of my lease, I have had only the occasional opportunity to reduce the coon population. Those have usually gone poorly, and not for the coon.

As turkey counts plunged further, I was spurred to action. I redoubled my efforts. I recorded the events. I tried to re-create the recipe Faulkner might have used to make coon palatable. If coon was proved tasty, I thought, others might join my chase with vigor. Florida backwoods chef Chip Turknett volunteered to turn a P. lotor into coon cuisine, but this required that I capture a P. lotor, not always a simple task. To complicate matters further, I use a longbow. I was hopeful of success on the chase and in the kitchen. I should have known better.

  Across Florida's lush green middle, cypress trees sprout from shallow pools in the pastures, making natural cabanas against the brutal summer sun. Cows crowd these overhangs during the day. Deer take their turn at dusk. Raccoons skulk in these hides too, creatures of the wet slough and saddle, rarely out in full light. To hunt deer or hogs here in the gloaming is to see raccoons at the water's edge, foraging with their human-like hands. As one grasps a grub and washes it before supper, he seems more like your Uncle Frank come-to-dinner than the terrorist he truly is. It takes a dedicated huntsman to target these masked marauders when they look so ... personable. But with our resolve in one hand and longbows in the other, my wife Karen and I set out to do just that.

  We drove our fields at dusk, bows strapped to our buggy, glassing for the bandit mask and banded tail of *Procyon lotor*. We found one digging along a cypress head, likely upending a freshly laid nest of eggs. Karen flung the door and leapt without a plan, excited, running, sure the coon was hers. I watched as she stalked and shot three times. The coon dodged each arrow with a deft twitch of its hip or a sharply raised paw, barely taking notice. He waddled into the oaks, Karen in hot pursuit. I found her later in the deep woods, staring up. The raccoon stared down. They were at a standoff until she drew overhead. If life was a movie, a rumbling score would have warned me to run.

  It did not occur to me then that standing under an agitated coon as I aimed a camera upward would be a poor plan. It did not occur to me then that Karen's arrow would knock the coon from the branch toward my face below, its legs akimbo, arms flailing, claws raking the air for my eyes. Unlike raccoons, I am slow to catch up with events around me.

Karen shot, the coon leapt, and I fell. My finger fired the camera like a turret gun all the way to the ground. We bounced in the dirt together, the raccoon barely missing my head before it ran off. Karen gave chase. I stayed down, feeling my sore hip for fractures. When I stood the sun had set. No coons or wives were in sight. I limped back to the buggy, finding my wife's arrows along the way by flashlight. I checked each for blood, hair or other signs of contact. There were none. Karen returned in the dark and stiffly took her seat, refusing to discuss the matter. The raccoon, I presumed, got away as clean as her arrows.

We retired the day but not the idea. We renewed the plan with a vengeance at dawn. Pigs, deer and turkey scattered in our wake. We were after coons. We rousted cypress heads and oak bottoms for hours without a sign, then sat for lunch, dejected. But before we had even unwrapped a sandwich, three banded tails loped across our path. Karen charged after them. They all scampered up the same small maple. I held back, wondering if the exponential risk of three airborne coons was worth taking. But these were ignorant teenagers, not suicide bombers. Karen had three coons cornered, if a tree can be said to have corners. We picked them off with our longbows and quickly moved all three from a maple branch to the game pole and a date with Chef Turknett.

Chip is a disciplined outdoor chef, not some drive-by saucier. He had done his homework. But while the old hands in camp allowed as how they might have heard that someone ate a coon once, maybe, and probably because they had to, none of them had actually tried one. Or would admit to it. Recipes for eel, otter, skink and skunk abounded, but not coon. We were on our own.

Wild meat has a mixed reputation, although some reviews should be flavored with a grain of cultural salt. What is and isn't edible

*Author after a rare successful coon hunt, heading for a bad day at the grill.
Photo by Karen Campbell.*

Coons, Cuisine, & Counterinsurgency

often has as much to do with the taster's address as his or her taste buds. Wild pigs are a prize in Florida, while Australians leave them for the buzzards. Carp are fertilizer in the United States, but Asian sportsmen will take theirs and yours home for dinner. Even so, sometimes bad is just bad. Some critters, no matter who or where you are, were just never meant to be eaten. Raccoon, I was beginning to think, just might fit that category.

Chip feared the worst, so borrowed from recipes designed for pig's butt and cow's neck, notoriously tough cuts. He marshaled every tender trick for one combined assault on the meat. He brined, parboiled, vinegar soaked and papaya rubbed it, pounded, sugared, steamed and seared it, cooked it low and slow, and ladled, slathered and injected it with glazes, rubs, and jellies. Karen and I monitored the action with strong brown drink in hand, occasionally handing one to the chef, occasionally pouring one on the meat. The coon smelled good and looked great, but so do ladies in Vegas.

Caveat Emptor, Chip and I thought. We called for a taster, but none of the old hands would step forward. I began to think that just maybe they knew more about eating coons than they had let on. Finally, bribed with drinks of rum and ginger sugar, Karen took the challenge. She sat before a grand platter of Coon au Poivre on greens and fruit, steadied by a robust Merlot, and cut into a new chapter in hunting camp fare.

There never was a full bite, not a complete chew through the meat. Not for lack of trying. The knife and fork pierced it, but the raccoon was beyond the strength of human teeth. Karen passed it from one molar to the other until finally her jaw just gave out. Chip worked a piece over too, but the coon couldn't be broken, even in death. We sliced it thinner, but like a rubber band the elasticity remained no matter the size. We had failed.

Chip still has two coons in the freezer, and hopes for new technology to someday make raccoon meat edible. I have no such illusions. Faulkner, if he ever ate raccoon, must have built those never-ending sentences to avoid sitting down for dinner. A sounder of hogs lives near our camp, and rumbles through the trash at night. Nothing organic is ever left, only cans, plastic and pans. Hogs are omnivores, after all. We threw that raccoon, so lovingly prepared, on the pile for the hogs to render. But in the morning, the carcass was still whole on a pile of plastic and tin cans, untouched.

Not even a pig, it seems, will eat a raccoon.

Hopelessly Helping

The boy stood behind me, gangly and too tall and all of twelve, watching a wild boar swirl and twist and throw his first arrow loose in a storm of dust under a grandfather oak. He was breathless from excitement, not exhaustion. A better hunter, maybe a better father or better guide, would have drawn an arrow and anchored the pig in place, ending things then and there. But I stood and gawked like a country rube at a carnival. I was the one anchored in place, helpless.

"You hit him!" I whisper-shouted, if such a thing is possible. I still didn't believe it, but the proof danced in front of me on cloven hooves.

"Yeah!" Cody blurted, leaning out to look around me, holding my coat, forgetting our rules about "hunting voices." The pig bucked and twirled once more and ran off, plopping away into the deep swamp. It wasn't hurt, only surprised, but not as much as I was.

"Wow."

"Yeah."

He spoke to me then as if I were his friend more than his father. But as his father I wondered if his first hunting strike would be

*Jay and Cody Campbell with a young pig taken by the author while teaching hunting to his son.
Photo by Karen Campbell.*

a good thing in his young eyes. In my day boys of twelve were natural predators. But this was Cody's day. Nature had long since been digitally wrapped and delivered to city boys, which my son had become after my divorce. This hunting encounter was his first. It wasn't life or death, but it was close, and I couldn't guess how he would react.

He looked up into my eyes, wide-eyed and grinning. He showed his braces, which was rare. His hand still held my coat. "That was better than a roller coaster!" He blurted out again, in full throat. "That was the best!" He couldn't contain his excitement. *Yes it was*, I thought, *for both of us*. My question had been answered without asking. Wow was right. I felt like taking a spin under the oak myself.

We found his arrow, barely bloodied by a pink inch of penetration. We followed the trail until the tracks sank ever deeper in the mud and we lost them to the black water. For all intents and purposes, the boar was uninjured. We drove through the swamp to camp. Cody's Uncle Matt was in the back seat, beaming, taking credit for the whole thing since he had seen the pig first.

Dinner at camp was a backslapping fest of old jokes about my young son, the sudden darling of rough men in a gentle rite of passage. The afternoon's events may have lacked the traditional substance for celebration, but given his late start in the woods Cody was graded on a curve. His first strike was ruled suitable for an initiation. Under a hunter's moon old friends hazed my young boy into our fading fraternity. I sat in the shadows, never closer to my son than I was on that afternoon.

Cody is my youngest child, which burdens him with the unfinished expectations of my life as well as his own. As fathers do, although we shouldn't, I look to my last boy for redemption. For mistakes made with him and my other children, for time not spent after school, conversations never had. I hold him tighter and miss him more because he is my last, although I can't put it into words. I have never known what to say. Not even when words were important.

"I'm leaving, buddy," I whispered, years ago. I sat on the edge of his cowboy bunk, waiting for a cab. I held my head in both hands. I looked at my feet. He wiped his sleepy eyes with one arm of his cartoon pajamas. The other held my coat. "I'm taking a new job," I said. The words stuck in my throat, and my fingers and face were wet. "I have to work in California, and I can't live here anymore." It wasn't a lie, but it was close, and I couldn't guess how he would react.

"When will I see you again?" he asked. He looked up into my eyes, wide-eyed and worried. His lip trembled, which was rare. The cab honked. I tried to stand, but his hand still held my coat. "I'll see you soon," I whispered, which was a lie, and I hugged him hard and I left, all wadded up inside. I was never farther from my son than I was on that morning.

In the years that followed I saw him once a month at most. He came to me wherever I was, wherever I had a job. I worked to be his father again, more than a driveway dad. I had taken something from him. I wanted to give it back. I wanted him with me.

I found a camp in the woods near his Florida house. We began to spend our monthly visits there. I piled that camp high with boy-sized guns, bows, reels and rods, even a slingshot. I hoped he would take up those old-school tools of the outdoors and close the gap between us. No such instant alchemy occurred. Cody did not become a country-wise nimrod overnight, but he showed a passing interest in the longbow. So we walked the woods on our weekends now and then, bows in hand. He reflected my lost youth. I mirrored what he might become.

"When will I see you again?" he asked when I dropped him at his mother's, stopped at the curb for a moment. A curtain pulled back inside, marking the time. He had to go. "Soon," I answered, which was a lie, and I left, wadded up inside.

It was never my plan to teach my boy the proper pursuit of pigs. I'm not sure there are such standards for pork in the south, not even guidelines. But stands of oaks edged the swampy pastures of our camp, and wild pigs filled our shallow brown sloughs. In those dark haunts, where palmetto fans and Spanish moss met to hide the light, a fidgety boy and his doting old man found wild hogs whether we wanted to or not.

When pigs happened, we huddled together and made plans to chase them. I took the lead. He tucked in behind me, happy. But if my job was to teach the Zen of pigs, I failed. Hogs usually escaped me in a mad passel of squeals and grunts, and left Cody laughing. I was interested in my boy, not the game.

Hunting returned my son to me. It let us speak without struggling over words. He wanted hunting arrows; I matched a set to his bow. He needed a quiver; I strapped one to his limbs with duct tape. We speared leafy targets in the field and skipped serious practice altogether. I fussed over his boy-sized gear more than my own, and I kept his arrows sharp. But for all the preparation and time afield, I never thought my PlayStation boy would actually shoot a pig. He seemed so young.

The day Cody shot at that first pig under the oak it was Uncle Matt who called him out from the back seat of my truck, not me. "Cody, get your bow." I was more surprised than my son. But Cody took the lead and I tucked in behind him, happy. The big oak covered us as he crawled close. He stood and drew. He was serious; intense; deadly. I smiled and knelt in the grass, ready to jump up and console him when he missed. Instead, I stood open-mouthed as Cody's dart danced in the pig's chest and then flew free.

There is a coming of age, a time usually prescribed by years, when our children become real to us in their own right and not only as our offspring. I remember sharply the day my father first spoke to me as if I were something more than his kid. That afternoon was Cody's time. He became something more to me than my son. I became more to him than his father. We were partners in the woods that day, more like brothers.

He changed after that. He focused on the hunt. He asked for a stronger bow. I delivered it in days, matched with hunting arrows. He began to practice. He went out with the other men in camp when I was busy, to learn the proper pursuit of pigs.

The Florida summer begins in May, ending our season. Cody had not yet taken an animal. In the rising heat, pigs had become scarce. On our last night we walked the wet edges of the oaks into an evening wind. Cody took the lead. I nagged him about noise as he stumbled and

Cody Campbell with his first pig, taken with a longbow, from 10 yards on the ground with one arrow. A very proud moment for Cody and his dad.

snapped twigs. I thought it was hopeless. But a light rain made the walking quiet, and we settled down to wait with the wind in our faces.

The setting sun lit a yearling pig from behind. It stepped into the pasture alone. Cody tried to stand, but I still held his coat. He looked back and smiled and I let him go, feeling silly. He seemed a head taller than just a month before. He seemed to be someone else's boy. He stepped into the pasture alone, judging the wind and cover. He was beyond needing me.

His arrow flew, and I held my breath. The pig crumpled in place. Then I ran and hugged my son hard. I never wanted to leave that field and that moment. But I couldn't put it into words. I have never known what to say, even when words were important.

We parked at his mother's curb for a moment. He reached for the door. "I'm coming back, buddy," I said softly. The words came easier this time. "I'm moving back to be with you again." He turned and looked up into my eyes, wide-eyed and grinning. I pulled him close and felt his face against my chest. "When will I see you again?" he asked. His words were muffled in my shirt. "Soon," I said, but this time it was true.

That was better than a roller coaster, I thought to myself, as I left him alone for the last time. *That was the best.*

Longbow

Archer's Paradox is Jay Campbell's upcoming novel, expected Fall 2013.

This is Chapter One.

Archer's Paradox

Chapter One

A clean edge, that's all I need, he thought. Just an edge on the cliff where this snowbound wall of branches and brambles will give way to the light. Just a place where I can get to a bluff and see the river, maybe find a way to climb down. A way to climb down before this damn snow kills me or Marty pushes off with the raft, which is pretty much the same thing.

His heart pounded in his chest, then again in his left boot. The left boot held his ankle together. It was seven hours now since he fell, then bound his foot up and jammed it back in the calf-high Wolverine. Some fall. Twelve hundred miles from home to skid six inches off a goose-crap slippery log, catch his ankle, and fall with his full weight against the joint. It snapped like a pine twig in a fire. At least he had codeine along. But codeine couldn't make the foot work again, and it made thinking a fuzzy chore.

The snow was falling hard now, piling up thick and wet and fast. The temperature was still dropping as well, and Marty might not wait to push off. There'd be no easy way out of here if the river froze any more, and this storm would ice it up good by morning. *Go on Marty, you jerk,* he thought, *Get out tonight and leave me alone in Alaska, one hundred miles from nowhere.*

Archer's Paradox

"Big" Conner was in a situation. His dream trip had been a nightmare from the start, seven miserable days ago. And now, just when he thought it couldn't get any worse, it had. *At least,* he thought, *when I die up here this damn trip will finally be over.* He had won the Alaskan float trip at an Elk Foundation Banquet last summer. The price was right and it sounded perfect —two weeks rafting the Stone River in Alaska, hunting bear with wooden bows and arrows. Finally he would be in the real wilderness, one hundred miles from anything that walked on two legs. Except for Marty McCann.

The outfitter had paired him up blindly with Marty. They met for the first time in Anchorage. Big realized pretty quick the trip wasn't free—the price was two weeks with Marty, God's gift to the great outdoors. Marty was the kind of guy who looked down on everyone around him—mostly, it seemed, because they weren't Marty. In less than an hour, Big learned that Marty had taken more game, made more money, and been with more women than any man alive. The hunting and women claims were a joke (Marty was a squat three hundred pounds, with half of it hanging over his belt), but he sure had the money. Every piece of Marty's gear was the best: the Black Widow bow, Randall knife, and the form-fitted Russell boots. He made sure Big knew it, too. Until this miserable trip, Marty always got the best of everything.

A few minutes after the Piper Cub dropped them on a gravel bar, Big and Marty knew they'd both been screwed. The more gear they unpacked, the worse things looked. Instead of the promised five-man tent, they had a tiny two-man, with burn holes through the fly. The rafts looked like D-Day surplus, and neither one would hold air. There was a repair kit, but it took every patch just to make one old Avon float. Big found a crack in the stove's burner when it flared up and seared his face. The only thing that might have worked was the Coleman lantern, but they never got to try it—the mantles were missing. Even worse, Big's

Chapter One

.44 Magnum pistol didn't make it to camp. It was probably still on the plane with the outfitter. Big was kicking himself for not checking the inventory when they unloaded. Now they had no choice but to float the river to the take out point, two weeks and one hundred miles away. Things looked bad for the trip, even if the clear weather had held.

But it didn't. It rained in sheets on day one, and it had rained or snowed every day since, until last night. With the best of gear, hunting would have been almost impossible, but at least they could have stayed warm and dry. Instead, the leaking tent pooled water like a bathtub and there were no tarps to jury-rig a shelter. Everything was soaked or frozen, day and night, including Big and Marty. So they stayed wet, even in their sleeping bags, and they kept all their clothes on, all the time.

Even so they had to curl up like newlyweds to keep from freezing at night. Big was cold and cramped, and it made him queasy to be pressed up against Marty like that. He didn't sleep much. During the day they kept moving to stay warm, floating the river early and scouting in the afternoon. They never saw game. The bears were probably holed up, waiting out the storms. But since Marty never stopped talking, never stopped complaining, and never let Big out of his sight, it didn't matter. Any game was long gone by the time they got there, and Big was getting sick of it.

That's why Big was alone this morning, miles away from Marty. Rain or not, they would have to float the river every day to make the take-out point in two weeks. But in seven days, there never had been a real chance to hunt. The afternoon forays were only to keep moving and stay warm. Big couldn't stand it—to be finally here, in the real wilderness, and not hunt at all. Then last night the sky had broken clear. Big wanted to hunt before it closed in again, and he wanted to hunt alone. The mountains swept up steep from both sides of the water, giving Big a chance for bear high up on the slopes.

Marty hated the idea. He wanted to keep floating the river and get out of Alaska before something else went wrong. But Big had to hunt the wilderness at least once. And he wanted solitude, even if it was dangerous. In the early dark, Big climbed into the mountains while Marty stayed in camp. He promised to be back by noon to get on the river, but beyond that there was no plan. They weren't talking much anymore. By sunrise Big was four or five miles away, high above the river. An hour later, the snow blew in again, and the temperature began to drop. By 10:00 am Big's ankle was broken, and it was already ten degrees colder. Now there was just an hour until dark and Big was afraid Marty would leave him behind, if he hadn't already.

The morning's plan seemed pretty stupid when he thought about it. But morning was a long time ago, before Big's new cedar arrows broke in the fall, and before his best self-made longbow became a half-assed crutch. He was so far from camp Marty could never find him. Hell, Big himself didn't even know where he was. All he knew was that he was downriver from camp but too far away to get back on his own. To make things worse, the light would fade soon and he couldn't find a clear place to look down at the water. *At least,* he thought, *I know where the river is.* His ankle grated and throbbed with each hopping step, so he took some more codeine. He had taken quite a bit to keep him moving—anything to ease the pain.

Big knew a cliff overlooking the river was close—maybe fifty yards away. He had taken a bearing on the river valley from a high slope an hour ago, then hobbled down until the bush got too thick. He was close, but he had an icy knot of trees, brambles, and bushes to get through. The vegetation was like a fortress wall with the cliff's edge protecting the river. It was too high and too wide to cross or go around, so there was only one option —go through. At the snowline, Big could see small openings—the tops of tunnels in the vegetation used by rab-

Chapter One

bits, wolverines, and other small game. He dropped down and dug the snow away from the biggest one, excavating down maybe two feet to the ground beneath the thicket.

The tunnel was good sized, and covered a well worn trail for the smaller animals. Big was no small animal, but he took his bearings and crawled in hands first. Where the tunnel closed in, he cut it wider with a buck knife. It was slow, cold going. Every time he cut a branch, snow flopped down, covering his head. His belly and legs were already soaked through from sliding along the ground, and he was frozen to the bone. An inch at a time, he pulled himself through with his elbows and arms, dragging his bow and quiver along. His left foot was useless now, just dead weight behind him.

The farther in he went, the darker it became. He felt like the sun had gone down, but it was too early for that. If the sun did set, he might as well stay in the thicket—it was as good a place to die as anywhere else. One thing was sure, it was still getting colder. After ten yards or so, he tired and slowed down, then just lay quiet. The codeine was making him sleepy. He thought about how good it would be to rest, but his own shivering and his chattering teeth kept him awake. Still, he just lay there.

Then he heard it. A low static noise that he could only hear lying there quietly—the dull roar of a fast river. Big couldn't work faster, he could hardly work at all. But he was inspired to move and cut again, and crawl to the sound. Within a few yards the tunnel brightened and opened up wide. He pulled himself free into the light.

In front of him was the Stone River Valley, wide and free. All of Alaska was collected below him. But when he crawled through the snow and peered over the edge, his gut turned. Even if he could keep moving, there was no way to get there from here. It was two hundred feet to the water, all of it straight down—a shear drop.

Archer's Paradox

The snow began to ease up and Big had a clear view of the river. It was colder now, well below zero. Damn if the water didn't flow straight under him. It built up some heavy rapids, too. He could see the white tops snapping over the rocks and ice, and hear the roar. It was loud, even this high. Then the water turned away and widened, and eased out from under him, nice and slow. If things weren't so damn desperate, this would have been a beautiful spot. He could see miles of mountain ridges running on both sides of the river, all white and glossy smooth and untouched. Finally, this was it, the real wilderness. What a way to find it.

Big looked upstream and startled a bit when he saw color on the river. Marty! The son of a bitch was on the water, leaving him behind. After a week on the river, Big knew Marty would never hear a shout or whistle from so high with the rapids running the way they were. The .44 Mag might have cut through, but that was wishful thinking now. He had to try something. His fanny pack had a "world's loudest" whistle from LL Bean, and a space blanket made of super thin aluminum foil. Maybe Marty would see the blanket. Big's frozen hands could barely pull the zipper on the pack. He was so cold that when he pulled on the metal tab, his whole hand shook up and down, jerking the zipper with it. There was just no picking things out from the pack with those trembling hands so he dumped it all over in the snow to find what he needed.

Finally he had the whistle in his mouth and blew as best he could, but the sound was faint, even to him. His teeth chattered on the plastic mouthpiece. While he blew he tried to unfold the space blanket, but it wouldn't separate. Like his other emergency gear, the blanket was five or six years old, and had fused together. It started coming apart in strips, little pieces that stuck to his fingers. He finally threw it over the edge, almost down to the river. His whole body was shivering now. Big

Chapter One

watched the ball of foil sail down to the gravel bank while he blew and blew on the whistle. But when he saw the foil bounce, he stopped. Hell, he realized, I can almost hit the water from here.

And then he had a plan.

Marty was coming into the bend faster now, so there wasn't much time. Big dragged himself to his feet. He looked for something to throw but there was nothing but branches and snow. And his bow. Marty wasn't looking up, and couldn't hear the damn whistle, but Big could send a message with that beautiful longbow. The raft picked up speed now, heading into the rapids. There was almost no time. Big leaned back on a tree trunk, then reached into his quiver. Eleven of a dozen handmade arrows had broken when he fell, and he had thrown those out this morning. The broken pieces had made a bright-colored pile on the snow, like old Christmas ornaments. But there was one arrow left.

Big had done this kind of shooting for years, down and up hills for fun. Fifty, seventy-five yards—stump shooting. But never at this distance, never at a moving target, and never with so much on the line. It would be maybe 150 yards. He had to get Marty's attention, which meant dropping an arrow in front of the raft. It wouldn't work when Marty was in the rapids. The raft was going too fast and Marty would be distracted. No, he had to wait until the raft turned and headed away, wait until it was slowing into the bend. The shot would be easier then, too. If he could align the flight of the arrow with the raft heading away, all he had to do was get the distance right. And get close enough to get Marty's attention. It would be a hell of a shot to even get it close.

Big started to feel woozy from standing, and his ankle pounded like a piston. Soon, he thought, those extra codeine would kick in and take care of the ankle. He shook out the cobwebs in his head and pulled the arrow from the quiver. The raft slipped through the last of the rapids and he could see Marty let up on the oars—no need to steer in the calm water. The bow arc'd back, and Big took in the mountains on the other side of the river and the bobbing raft, all stretching out in front of that sharp-edged broadhead. He clenched every muscle to keep from shivering, from shaking the arrow from the bow. Then he let fly. The arrow raced out over the water, then fell off slowly, dropping down to the river, bright red feathers spinning tightly. It looked perfect, and it closed on the raft like a rocket.

It seemed to take forever, long enough for Big to realize again how cold he was, and how tired he was. Long enough to realize he needed to lie down or faint. But he watched the feathers spin to the target, and it looked perfect. It might just work, he thought, it's going to drop right in front of the raft. Damn, what a shot! He even started planning how to get down from the edge with Marty's help. Then . . . oh crap! He watched Marty stand up to pull on an oar. *Damn, Marty, Sit down!* he thought. *It'll pass over if you sit down.* Marty stepped up to the bow of the raft. Sit down! But the arrow and Marty came together like old friends.

The shaft hit, and Marty dropped the oar and looked down at the length of arrow protruding from his breast. Big knew there was a sound, but he couldn't hear it. And then Marty fell over in the raft, his head hanging over the side in the water. The Avon spun in aimless circles downstream, trailing streaks of blood. Big started to shiver again, his whole body shaking. *Hell,* he thought, *poor Marty.*

Big was suddenly tired, very tired. He slumped down the tree trunk and sat in the snow, then just lay down to sleep for the last time. He was in the real wilderness at last, one hundred miles from anything that walked on two legs. What a way to leave it.

Alone in the wilderness, where no one could see, Big smiled just a bit before he slept. Poor Marty, he thought. But that shot—that

Chapter One

was a hell of a shot. *Yeah,* he thought, and then he didn't think anymore *... a hell of a shot.*

That was the shot of a lifetime.

Doc Scarborough had run the Alaska Regional Emergency Room for thirty years, and thought he'd seen it all - until now. Big was lucky to be unconscious. He wouldn't have appreciated the warm enema that was bringing his frozen body back to room temperature. He was better off asleep, not feeling the sensation of razors burning his flesh as blood pulsed back into his frostbitten face and right hand.

Big was still in a situation. Pieces of him were going to be cut away soon to save his life, and Prosecutor Nanni Stone wanted to lock up whatever was left - forever. The helicopter had brought two bodies in on the same trip. Marty McCann's bloated corpse was in the basement morgue, getting almost as much attention as Big. No one could recall a white man killed with an arrow before. Or a native, for that matter.

As Doc Scarborough forced life into Big's remains, the coroner dissected Marty McCann's, and the ripples around Big's last arrow grew wider and faster than anyone could have imagined. Anyone, that is, except Dot Pultrow, the editor, copy girl, and only employee of the *Anchorage Weekly Herald*.

When the scanner on Dot's kitchen table first cracked with the news of the gruesome airlift near Stoney river, Dot traded her housecoat and vinyl dinette for a coyote lined parka, a set of tight black stretch ski pants, and the frosty cab of her 1975 Toyota pickup. When the rescue chopper wobbled to a landing she was waiting, and she had been pounding the pavement and her typewriter keys ever since. Dot was determined to make the death of Marty McCann the biggest story in the history of the *Weekly*.

The API picked up Dot's byline the next morning, and it became a big story for the rest of the country as well. Especially in Sarasota, Florida, where Marty McCann's twin sons had just received the news. Bullet and Tracer McCann weren't taking Marty's death well, and they didn't plan to take it in Sarasota at all. By noon they had flights booked to Anchorage to do their grieving in person. Judging by the contents of their checked bags, one might have thought the twins planned to do some hunting, too.

Jay and Karen Campbell beginning a new adventure on their 50 foot Trawler, Largo, bearthed in Florida.

CODA

Karen and I bought a boat, a big one, and filled it with cameras and computers and not much more. Friends think we've lost our senses. We may have. Our hunting life is on hold as we make ready to live on an ocean, any ocean, if it's passably warm. The Atlantic is closest. Our fifty-foot, three deck, thirty-year-old trawler *Largo* is home base now. We dream of long lines and lee shores, gentle swells and calm seas, but we'll settle for the southern horizon and the islands beyond.

Our next book may be: "Trawler: Hunting a Life on the Sea". We hope to share it with you.

"Wrote a note said be back in a minute,
Bought a boat and sailed off in it"

"Knee Deep in the Water" - Zac Brown and Jimmy Buffett

Longbow

About the Author

Jay Campbell has been hunting with the longbow since he was nine. He has been a professional musician, photographer, police officer, paramedic, physician's assistant and firefighter, is a practicing attorney, and has directed organ procurement and transplant organizations throughout the U.S. since 1989. A cancer survivor, he graduated Duke University (*Magna Cum Laude*) and the University of North Carolina - Chapel Hill Law School (*With Honors*).

Karen Campbell is a former fashion model and a third-degree black belt instructor in Shotokan. She was trained in classical piano and flute at the *Academie de Musique* in Belgium and is president of her own computer programming company. Karen had never hunted or held a bow when she and Jay married. This book, in part, recounts her two year journey to become the first woman known to take a water buffalo with a longbow, using her 70 pound bow from the ground on Australia's Melville Island.

The Campbells have seven children and two dogs between them, and live on Tampa Bay. A flats boat is tied behind their house and their fifty-foot, thirty year old trawler *Largo* is docked nearby, both ready to make way on the tides of opportunity or disaster.

Jay and Karen Campbell are on-line at www.jaycampbellphotography.com, where their books, projects, photographs and adventures are available and irregularly updated.

PRESS

Raven's Eye Press
Rediscovering the West
www.ravenseyepress.com

Have Bow, Will Travel: Around the World Adventure with Longbow and Recurve
by E. Donnall Thomas, Jr.

Language of Wings
by E. Donnall Thomas, Jr.

Racks: A Natural History of Antlers and the Animals That Wear Them
by David Petersen

Ghost Grizzlies: Does the Great Bear Still Haunt Colorado?
by David Petersen

Heartsblood: Hunting, Spirituality, and Wildness in America
by David Petersen

Visit www.ravenseyepress.com
for a complete listing of our titles.

CPSIA information can be obtained at www.ICGtesting.com
Printed in the USA
LVOW061014101212

310787LV00002BB/3/P